Bargain S

In Palm Beach County

Plus Broward & Miami

The 150 Best Consignment, Thrift, & Vintage Shops for Home Décor, Furnishings, Antiques, Clothing, Jewelry, Handbags & Shoes

(Plus malls, outlets, flea markets, estate sales and shopping centers)

---

by

Paulette Cooper Noble

The Happy Shopper

www.shoppinginflorida.net

BARGAIN SHOPPING IN PALM BEACH COUNTY
Plus Broward & Miami

The 150 Best Consignment, Thrift, & Vintage Shops for Home Décor, Furnishings, Antiques, Clothing, Jewelry, Handbags & Shoes

(Plus malls, outlets, flea markets, estate sales and shopping centers)

©2017 by Paulette Cooper Noble and Paul Noble
All rights reserved.

Published by: Polo Publishing of Palm Beach
Post Office Box 621
Palm Beach, FL 33480

ISBN: 978-0991401352

Printed in the United States of America

Photographs by Paulette Cooper Noble
Graphic Design by Mia Crews/ManuscriptFormatting.com
Polo photo by Lenny Hirschfield
Photos of Paulette & Paul by Tina Valant
www.shoppinginflorida.net

FACEBOOK: SHOPPINGINFLORIDA

To reach the author, E-mail *shopinpalmbeach@aol.com*

ACKNOWLEDGMENTS

Thanks especially to **SUSAN COLEMAN, ANDREW FLESCHNER** and **LISA PETERFREUND** for their research, ideas, and support, which made this and the earlier versions of this book possible. Most of all, to my wonderful husband, **PAUL NOBLE**, for patiently waiting while I worked 16 hours a day to write this book, and for (rightly) believing that I was out working when I was out shopping.

ഇ൭ൠ
DEDICATION

This book is dedicated to my father, TED COOPER, who lived to almost 100 without ever being inside a consignment, thrift or vintage shop.

TABLE OF CONTENTS

Author's Note

Some shoppers get pleasure when they spend money; others when they save it. If you belong to that second group, this book is for you. Some seek Salvation Army, others salvation in Armani.

Even before Cheap Chic became fashionable, many of you—sometimes secretly—had already discovered the joys of bagging a designer handbag at a consignment shop, of encountering a treasure in a thrift shop, of rediscovering a favorite gown at a vintage shop, or of finding a barely-used piece of furniture in a consignment store that fits perfectly into that lonely corner of your home. If this is you, this is a book for you.

There's something for everyone in this book whether its high-end consignments or rock-bottom thrifts where you can bag a bargain for a buck. (See Section IV for inexpensive thrift shops.) There are places where you can find the perfect accent for a piece in your home, and shops where you can buy all of the furniture for it.

This book is divided into geographical regions (Palm Beach, Broward & Miami), towns, and then the shops are listed alphabetically within them.

Every one of the 150+ stores was personally checked out by me at least once. I know what you're thinking. "Wow—she calls going to stores work?" But it was hard work. And now I'm glad to be finished with it, and I can do something for fun—like shopping.

In fact, in some ways, this book is like shopping: serendipitous. There is no index of stores in the back. I want people to skim through the sections and discover places they didn't know existed and then get in their cars and go to them. That's what makes shopping—and hopefully reading this book—fun.

But don't go overboard. Remember The Happy Shopper's motto: You don't have to spend a hundred to look like a million.

Paulette Cooper Noble
The Happy Shopper

1

Part I
Palm Beach County

ઋ૦ભ
Boca Raton

HIGH-END CONSIGNMENT SHOPS
FOR CLOTHING & FURNITURE IN BOCA

Within a small area near Mizner Park are two high-end women's consignment shops. Coming off of A1A, start at **ENCORE PLUS** at 281 E. Palmetto Park Road.

Then, continue west to Federal, go north, and then right a few blocks up to SE 2nd. There's a little mall where you'll find **RAZZAMATAZZ OF BOCA RATON** at 116 NE 2nd St.

For home décor, furniture, and gifts, **LEGACY ESTATE & HOME FURNISHINGS** at 2980 N. Federal Hwy., and **COCONUT CONSIGNMENT** at 68 S. Federal. Hwy., are both great. A description of all these shops is below along with additional Boca stores.

ઋ૦ભ

B. LOVELY CONSIGNMENT

www.blovelyconsignment.com; Facebook: B. Lovely Consignment
1000 N. Dixie Hwy. / Boca Raton 33432 / (561) 394-9325 / OPEN: Mon.-Sat. 10-5

You might think this new women's clothing shop got the name of B. Lovely because everything in it is lovely (and b-eautiful) and yes, that's true. But the owner's name is Brittney Lovely. So that also explains the B—and the Lovely.

Wherever the name came from, this is truly a lovely place with

2

carefully selected garments and accessories that range from affordable to Escada to…which is still affordable here. Her prices are amazing. Perfect condition Escada blouses, for example, were an incredible $42. A Judith Lieber bag that would easily go for a thousand plus elsewhere was $600. (That one was in one of four cases of accessories.) "I'm not that greedy that I need to charge a lot," explained Brittney. "I want everyone who walks into this store to be able to buy something." Toward that end, she stocks clothes that would sell at shops ranging from Macy's to Bergdorfs. How Lovely.

COCOBLUE

www.cocoblueboutique.com;
www.facebook.com/groups/cocoblueconsignment// 75 S. Federal
Hwy. /Boca Raton 33432 / (561) 367-7177 /
OPEN: Tues.-Sat.11-4

The great Cocoblue has moved from their old location, and now this old favorite is even more convenient on Federal in East Boca. The new incarnation—like the old store—is small but stylish with a very boutique-y feel about it. It's filled with mid-range and higher-end designer clothing, handbags, and shoes—in every shape, color, and size—plus jewelry and clothing of local designers. All guaranteed to spice up your wardrobe. Its name reflects its content: CocoBlue was named because they have everything from Coco Chanel to Blue Jeans. This cozy consignment shop has won a number of awards, and rightly so. They pack a lot in, without it seeming crowded. And the inventory is constantly changing. **NOTE:** There's a parking lot in the rear.

SHOP NEARBY: COCONUT CONSIGNMENT (see next entry) is across the street.

ဆာလ

You had me at the word "bargain"

—Anonymous

ဆာလ

COCONUT CONSIGNMENT COMPANY

68 S. Federal Hwy. / Boca Raton 33432 / (561) 362-7040 / OPEN: Mon.-Sat. 10:30-5

I've been a great fan of this shop for decades because it's a terrific furniture, home décor and gift shop that's easy to get to: it's one block south of Palmetto Park Road on Federal Highway.

It's a bit hard to get around the shop, though, because it's so full. But that's fine, because it gives you lots of great things to explore, and plenty of good things to buy.

Coconut Consignment's motto is "unusual things from unusual places," and they could have added "at unusual prices"—unusually low for this type of fine merchandise and all in practically pristine condition. And you'll find plenty here to upgrade or improve your place.

DON'T MISS: There's a small section to the right in the back with fun knick-knacks.

SALES INFORMATION: They always offer everything for 10% off.

CONSIGNMENT EXCHANGE

www.facebook.com/consignmentexchange // Shoppes at Boca Grove, 21073 Powerline Rd., Suite 23/ Boca Raton 33433/ (561) 852-7644 / OPEN: Mon. 11-4; Tues.-Fri. 10-6; Sat. 10-5

There's a reason I have been coming to this three-room heavily-

stocked shop for almost three decades. Even before I moved to Florida, when I would come here to visit relatives, I would immediately run to this place. I've been one of many faithful fans of a consignment shop that carries well-priced, gently-worn apparel and accessories for women of all ages. That also includes younger ones, which is unusual, since most women's consignment shops ignore this age group. (When I first started coming here, I belonged to that group too!)This was always one of the great women's clothing consignment

4

shops in Boca, and now it's twice as good, no three times as good since they added a third room.

Young people will find as much to please them here as will their older counterparts, including a large collection of designer blue jeans. Still, you don't have to be young or old to delight in everything here, with prices ranging from as low as $14 for hoop earrings to $600 for a Chanel worth so much more than that. Boutique clothes are mixed in, but they're mostly in the front section. The room in the back has even more clothes, handbags and shoes, and plenty to choose from in their 50% off rack.

As if all this wasn't enough, this is also Handbag Heaven! There's an impressive amount of beautiful handbags throughout (including some hard-to-find vintage ones) with all the big designer names you'd want as well as those in a lower price range. Their collection of designer shoes and designer glasses is also extensive and not that expensive.

NOTE: Visit their Facebook page to find out about their special sales—even though the prices are already fabulous.

DEBBIE RAND MEMORIAL THRIFT SHOPPE
Facebook: Debbie-Rand Memorial Thrift Shop // 903 Meadows Rd. / Boca Raton 33486 / (561) 395-2208 / OPEN: Mon.-Sat. 9-4; possibly Sun 12-4

"We've sold everything except airplanes, and that includes cars and even a cemetery plot," said a salesperson here. But the best things they sell at this large hard-to-find thrift shop are the women's clothes and accessories in their boutique where clothes are generally 50% off.

You may be rewarded by finding a few labels from some well-known designers there, although generally not in tip-top consignment-shop condition. Still, you won't pay those kinds of prices either for a Judith Leiber or Fendi bag, both of which have been bagged by savvy shoppers in their separate "better" area. Still, don't expect too much. I was told that the volunteer workers sometimes grab the good stuff first. But that's true in all these places, so you just have to be lucky.

ENCORE PLUS

www.facebook.com/EncorePlusInc; Instagram: EncorePlusIncBoca/
281 E. Palmetto Park Rd. / Boca Raton 33432 / (561) 391-3812 /
OPEN: Mon.-Fri. 10-6; Sat. 10-5

This "designer resale boutique" is one of the most upscale consignment shops in Southeast Florida. Their clothes come from some of the most sought-after designers in the world, and if you don't mind paying a little more for the quality, then Encore Plus is a place you won't want to miss. Most of the clothes and accessories here have supposedly been worn but you'd surely never know it.

This beautiful shop has two stunning owners with impeccable taste. Their clothes are all very luxurious; even their shoes especially are practically wearable art, making them a shoe-in for best high-end footwear. They also have a back section with sale items for the more budget- conscious high-end shopper.

EVELYN & ARTHUR'S SALE ANNEX II

www.evelynandarthur.com/stores // 2200 Glades Rd., Suite 504 /
Boca Raton 33431 / **561) 391-5602** / OPEN: Mon.-Sat. 10-5

Of their nine regular retail shops, four are in Palm Beach County (Palm Beach, Manalapan, Palm Beach Gardens, and Boca Raton). Now they've added a fifth one—which is the best of all since it's a sales annex! It's located in Glades Plaza, just west of I-95 at the intersection of Glades Road and NW 19th Street. Evelyn & Arthur's children—who are now running all their shops—have stocked this place with the same contemporary private-label clothing and accessories in their regular stores. **NOTE:** This is an especially good venue for those who prefer retail shops to resale ones. (Although a lot of resale is new.) NOTE: Evelyn & Arthur's is right near three of Palm Beach's most popular restaurants, Nick & Johnnie's, Testa's and Cucina Dell 'Arte.

ജോൽ
"If you don't believe one shoe can change your life, ask
CINDERELLA!
ജോൽ

THE 13 MOST UPSCALE (EXPENSIVE) WOMEN'S CLOTHING CONSIGNMENT & VINTAGE SHOPS IN PALM BEACH COUNTY

ෂාශ්

ANNEXE de LUXE (Palm Beach) • ATTITUDES (Palm Beach) • BALATRO VINTAGE (Palm Beach) • CLASSIC COLLECTIONS (Palm Beach) • DINA C'S FAB & FUNKY (West Palm Beach) • ENCORE PLUS (Boca Raton) • FASHIONISTA (Palm Beach) • JENNIFER'S DESIGNER EXCHANGE (Palm Beach Gardens) • MAXIMS OF PALM BEACH (Palm Beach) • PALM BEACH VINTAGE (West Palm Beach) • RAZAMATAZ (Palm Beach) • RAZZAMATAZ OF BOCA RATON (Boca Raton) • SERENDIPITY (Boca

EXQUISITE CONSIGNMENT

www.facebook.com/ExquisiteConsignment // 6455 N. Federal Hwy. / Boca Raton 33487/ (561) 350-9861/OPEN: Tues.-Sat. 10-4; Sat. 11-5

The gorgeous Mexican-born Marza formerly owned a popular jewelry booth at the **SAMPLE ROAD FLEA MARKET** in Broward County. But she was too classy for that, and her merchandise too elegant for them. Now, she has opened up a tiny jewel of a shop that's as beautiful as she is. Even though it's small, there's space for stunning resale couture clothes and costume jewelry for far less money than you would have paid at the market. Marza is also open to negotiation, saying that she wants to keep her customers happy and keep coming back.

SHOP NEARBY: Further south at 5781 North Federal Highway, you might find **VANDA CONSIGNMENT BOUTIQUE** open. Then too you might not. She has a wide range of merchandise and prices—a few really high-end items up front—but there's little organization

7

elsewhere. That also seems to be true of the owner. Her small shop is only open in the afternoons, if it's open, and if you go there and it's totally gone, don't say I didn't warn you. You might try calling first: (646) 346-9390.

GOODWILL BOCA BOUTIQUE

www.gulfstreamgoodwill.org // 1662 N. Federal Hwy. / Boca Raton 33432 / (561) 362-8662 / OPEN: Mon.-Sat. 9-7; Sun. 10-6

This is a surprisingly good thrift shop, and the housewares/gifts along with shoes are really good here. But the most outstanding buys are sitting in a glass case to the left when you enter, where you'll find a dozen or so high(er) end known-label handbags and shoes at "lower-end" prices. Even the less expensive shoes on the racks are worthwhile going through. Because every once in a while….bingo.

The furniture here is also sometimes several notches above what you'd find in most thrifts but the selection is small. Still, it was probably donated from a beautiful home in the area and won't cost anywhere near what they paid for it.

HOSPICE BY THE SEA CHEST THRIFT SHOP

Facebook: Hospice by the Sea Chest Thrift Shop // Plum Park / 141 NW 20th St. / Boca Raton 33486 / (561) 338-4030/ OPEN: Tue.-Sat. 10-4:30

This is now the lone thrift store in the back of Plum Plaza (LEVIS JCC is up front) and they've joined forces with the Hospice of Palm Beach County, which runs a terrific thrift shop in Juno Beach. (See Jupiter/Juno/Tequesta chapter.)

As a result, this once lackluster shop now has some very good men's clothes, furniture, and home décor. There's a large book and knick-knack area hidden to the right, where the Happy Shopper picked up an adorable Limoges plate for $5. As for clothes, some of the men's clothes in the back boutique is the best outside of a consignment shop—and there are few of those for men anyway. But you'll pay much less for much more here. As for the women's clothes, they're mostly disappointing. Still, you may find something so look all around. It's not as good as LEVIS JCC up front, but it's in the same mall so visit both.

LEGACY ESTATE & HOME FURNISHINGS

www.legacyfurnitureconsignment.com;
www.facebook.com/LegacyEstateLiquidationSales;
Instagram: legacy_home_furnishings_consig // 2980 N. Federal Hwy.
/Boca Raton 33431/(561) 409-2126/OPEN: Mon.-Sat. 10-6; Sun.12-5

Although this 10,000-square-room emporium also carries designer bags, costume jewelry, collectibles, and a fantastic selection of goods, the real stars here are the name-brand furniture. Owner Nancy Rosenthal carefully selects every piece of the gorgeous furniture that

comes in. The result is a showroom with pieces that are reminiscent of those you see in a top designer magazine. This shop will help you fulfill your decorating dreams—and there's room to walk around and marvel at it all. Especially the wonderful prices.

Go with a tape measure because you'll see much that's magnificent which you'll want to take home if it fits. (And if doesn't, some items are so great you'll be ready to move!) I'm forever falling in love with something there and then running home to measure the area where it might go. Besides offering beautiful estate furniture, they'll also help you plan and conduct your own estate sale.

LEVIS JCC THRIFT SHOP

www.levisjcc.org/shop / Plum Park / 141 NW 20th St. / Boca Raton 33431 / (561) 368-3665 / OPEN: Mon.-Sat. 10-5; Sun. 11-4

This is the second of the two great thrift shops in Plum Park, and hands down, they have the best merchandise. Not only in this mall but among thrift shops in general. Their prices are sometimes a bit higher than other thrifts, but they almost always offer 50% off everything which brings it down considerably. And there are some incredible buys for women and men's clothes in their boutique sections.

Bargains are all around. One shopper joyfully reported that during one of their many sales, she purchased her son-in-law a Christian Dior jacket, a Brooks Brother shirt, and Armani pants—all for $35.

They also usually carry some vintage clothes, some furniture, and also items that are not routinely carried by other thrift shops. For example, there's some Judaica in the back and sometimes in one of the glass showcases by the entrance.

SALES INFORMATION: Everything in the store over some small amount (like $1-$5) is usually 50% off, and sometimes they have additional sales over that.

ॐ

"Shopping is a woman thing. It's a contact sport like football. Women enjoy the scrimmage, the noisy crowds, the danger of being trampled to death, and the ecstasy of the purchase."

—Erma Bombeck

ॐ

THE CAT'S MEOW—LITERALLY

A woman in Washington couldn't figure out where the strange sounds she heard at night were coming from. She began to wonder if it could be related to the couch she had purchased in a consignment shop a few weeks earlier. She took the couch apart... and inside was a noisy surprise. It seems a cat had crawled into the couch through a small hole.

The news story on her furry find led to the owner of the cat being found. The owner had been moving and her cat had disappeared—apparently hiding in the couch. The cat was returned to her. What happened to the dismantled couch was not reported.

NINE WAYS TO TELL IF A DESIGNER HANDBAG (CHANEL, VUITTON, BURBERRY, ETC.,) IS REAL

People used to sell bags stamped "Goochi," or fake Rolexes whose second hands moved spastically instead of smoothly so everyone knew they weren't real. Now it's often impossible to tell if a product is counterfeit. (Actually, a fake may look *better*, since many real bags are made by hand and fakes by machines.) But here are some tip-offs that may help you tell if an expensive "designer" handbag is real.

1. See if the pattern aligns correctly. For example, look at the Burberry bag stripes on the seams (and where the bag opens). There should be a continuation of the pattern. In a quilted Chanel, the top triangle should continue below the flap. When you close the bag, the bottom of the triangle should smoothly blend in so it's a real triangle. Check the lining, which is where counterfeiters often scrimp to save money. Not only should it not look cheap, but you shouldn't be able to pull it away from the sides easily.

2. Look at the embossing or monogramming of the name, which should be very clean, clear and straight. Take the Burberry knight, for example. He should be defined and look like a knight with a lance on a horse. (Fakes have horses that may look fat and slightly out of shape.) The alligators on a real Lacoste will have stitching that clearly shows the animal's teeth.

3. Check the hardware. Make sure the zipper moves smoothly and doesn't catch, and that it doesn't feel light and cheap—and like plastic. And make sure the hardware is all the same color and finish.

4. Watch out for incomplete logos. A dead giveaway that a Vuitton is fake, for example, is if the LV is cut. Louis Vuitton doesn't cut away part of their logo, say when the letters reach the seam. Nor would they be interrupted by a zipper.

5. Patterns should mirror themselves. For example, on a Vuitton, if one end has two stars and two circles and an LV, you'll have the same configuration on the other side of the handbag.

6. If the bag comes with a booklet or card, it should not be photocopied.

7. Smell it. Leather should not smell like glue or chemicals.

8. Trust your instinct. If I wonder if it's real, it probably isn't; when it's real I look at it and know. Tami Rowe of CITY GIRL has another method: "If my heart starts fluttering, then it's a real Chanel."

9. Finally, if it's too inexpensive, it probably isn't real.

PAST PERFECT

www.pastperfectconsignment.com; Facebook: Past Perfect Consignment / 99 NE Mizner Blvd. / Boca Raton 33432 / (561) 338-5656 / OPEN: Mon.-Sat. 9:30-5:30; Sun. 12-5

This large five-room shop one block south of Mizner Park has been around for 32 years, and has some nice furniture, art, and decorative home accessories. They also sell some especially good costume jewelry, which may be reduced if it's been there for over a month.

NOTE: Past Perfect has a CLEARANCE CENTER at 1801 NW 1st. Ave. (561) 544-0950 for more information. Open Tues.-Sat., 10-5. **CONSIGNMENT SHOP NEARBY**: Razzamatazz of Boca Raton

PERFECTLY IMPERFECT

www.perfectlyimperfectconsignment.com; Facebook: Perfectly Imperfect Consignments / 3333 N. Federal Hwy., #2B, / Boca Raton 33431 / (561) 756-9267 / OPEN: Mon.-Sat. 10:30-5

The Happy Shopper has made many happy visits here because Perfectly Imperfect's home décor and gifts are more perfect than imperfect, and they carry unusual and unique consigned items in pristine condition.

Says the owner, Jennifer Gaffey: "We display them in a way people can envision the items in their own home."

The prices are really really good, and if you need a gift item, everything looks so new here that no one will know you paid anything less than retail for it. (Which, of course, you may not do anyway).

In addition to coffee table books, totes, a bit of estate jewelry, art, lighting and more, you'll occasionally find something pet-related. That's because owner Jennifer loves dogs, especially her tiny Madigan, the four-legged "Head of Security and Official greeter" who may welcome you when you come in.

RAZZAMATAZZ OF BOCA RATON

www.facebook.com/RazzamatazzBoca; Instagram: Razzamatazz_Boca_Raton // 116 NE 2nd St. / Boca Raton 33432 / (561) 394-4592 / OPEN: Mon.-Sat. 10-5

This small but beautiful high-end consignment boutique has some stunning merchandise. Just about everything there is top-designer gently-worn (or not-at-all-worn) clothes and accessories that look brand new. They don't have a lot of merchandise, but it's all quality clothes that will last for a long time.

They also have a large selection of designer jeans to the left—and sale items to the right. Two glass cabinets at the entrance are filled with posh designer handbags, and you'll find a few more in the case and behind the counter.

NOTE: It's just a block away from Mizner Park—and you'll probably get a better deal here.

SERENDIPITY

www.consignmentboca.com; Facebook: Serendipity Consignment // Glades Plaza / 2200 Glades Rd., Suite 506 / Boca Raton 33431 / (561) 338-0656 / OPEN: Mon.-Sat.10-5:30

This is probably Boca Raton's most high-end consignment—indeed, one of the most upscale in Southeast Florida. They were voted the #1 consignment shop by Boca Raton Magazine for almost ten years in a row. That's because the shop is spotless, and none of the beautiful clothes there are more than two years old. Indeed, when you walk in, you think you've accidentally ended up in one of the many women's retail clothing stores in this mall. And then when you're waited on by one of the three saleswomen! Well, you're sure that you're in the wrong place.

But you're not. You're here and you'll be glad. Especially when you see behind the glass the very upscale designer handbags, and the selection of real as well as costume jewelry, with names you know like Cartier, Hermes, Chanel, Bulgari, and Louis Vuitton, to mention a few.

In season, this super high-end women's clothing and accessories shop even carries a small rack of never-been-worn-looking furs, rare to see in a Florida consignment shop. (See Section V for more resales that carry fur.)

They run many spontaneous and unexpected sales at least once or twice a month, as well as semi-annual store wide sales for usually between 30 to 50 percent off. They also have a great layaway plan.

SHE'S SO SHABBY

www.shessoshabby.com; Facebook: She's So Shabby // 1720 NW 1st Ave. / Boca Raton 33432 / (954) 655-3937 / OPEN: Tues.-Sat. 11-5

This off-the-beaten street 3,000-square-foot showroom in an old War II army barrack is filled with painted shabby chic furniture as well as many one-of-a-kind items to decorate your cottage-style home. Adding to the feeling that you're definitely someplace different, their 1965 Wurlitzer jukebox may be playing as you stroll through the hand-painted vintage furniture, costume jewelry, mirrors, chandeliers, frames, windows and salvage.

This unique showroom is really a warehouse and painting studio combined. Jodi, the owner, will gladly custom paint and "shabby" your treasured or even your ordinary pieces, like kitchen cabinets.

You may think this casual place is somewhat shabby looking, but its content, as they say, is not too shabby.

SHOW & TELL CONSIGNMENTS & BOUTIQUE

www.showandtellconsignments.com; www.facebook.com/
ShowAndTellConsignments // 260 N. Dixie Hwy. / Boca Raton
33432 / (561) 391-1117 / OPEN: Mon.12-5; Tues.-Fri. 10:30-5:30;
Sat. 10–5; Sun. 12-4

When you walk in and see the stunning clothing and accessories, you think you've seen it all. But as you proceed to the next room, it opens up into a kiddy land. An adult land, actually, because it's a joy for both of you. I don't have children but I would almost want one just to outfit him or her in the great clothes in this shop.

Show & Tell is well situated, near Mizner Park, one block north of Palmetto Park Road. It's the largest (4,000 square feet—wow!) children's consignment shop in Boca, actually the largest for miles around. This huge emporium carries new and gently-used brand name items, starting from pregnancy garments right through to preteen.

They also sell harder-to-find school uniforms, dance and sports gear, dress-up and costume clothes, gifts, and baby shower presents. So come here and in one place, you can find all you need in clothes, furniture (strollers, cribs, bedding, plush outdoor pieces) baby gear, maternity, books, movies and toys, like Pack 'N Plays dolls, and battery-operated cars. And best of all, there's always a sale!

THE BEACH

www.shopthebeach.net;www.facebook.com/thebeachconsignment; Instagram@thebeachboutiqueboca // 3333 N. Federal Hwy. / Boca Raton 33431/(561)362-0234/OPEN:Mon.-Fri.10:30-5:30;Sat.10:30-4

The charming new owner, Kris, has taken over a popular old consignment spot, and it's even more of a treat coming here now—and it always was a great place. (Kris was a customer of the previous DZINES and loved it so much that she bought it!) Happily, she still carries must-buy clothes and accessories at an extremely affordable price.

The layout is uncomplicated, and there's plenty of room with everything nicely and neatly displayed so you can find what you want. In the back room, you'll see half-price racks and sometimes a "clearance corner" offering even bigger discounts. But whether it's a sale, or their regular resale, you can almost always find something here. That's why I always stop by when I'm anywhere nearby. I haven't always purchased something, but I would have if there was room in my closet for any of the lovely clothing and accessories at surprisingly low prices. Really!

SHOP NEARBY: PERFECTLY IMPERFECT CONSIGNMENTS

is right next door, and they carry stunning home décor, custom art, and gifts.

THE PURSE LADIES LLC

www.thepurseladies.com; www.facebook.com/The.Purse.Ladies // 21338 St. Andrews Blvd. / Boca Raton FL 33433 / (561) 962-5102 / OPEN: Mon.-Sat. 10-5

You're sure to bag a bargain in this small shop entirely filled with high-end pre-loved handbags, ranging from Coach to Chanel, from under $100 (not too many here) to …..

This unique shop, run by two sisters, already has many faithful fans. They line up not only for the handbags but for the make-up cases (I purchased a brand new $350 price-tag-still-on-it Fendi for $80), shoes, jewelry, sunglasses and other fun couture accessories.

They're not inexpensive, but they have an annual sale every October. Also, they guarantee the authenticity of all their items, which is reflected in their motto: "Designer Buyers You Can Trust."

TRI-COUNTY ANIMAL SHELTER THRIFT SHOP

www.tricountyhumane.org/thrift-shop / Plum Tree Center, 3350 NW 2nd Ave./ Boca Raton 33431 /(561) 338-4770 /OPEN: Tues.-Sat.10-4

The only thing wrong with the Tri County thrift shop is that it's hard to find. They've moved to Plum Tree Center, between Spanish River Road and 28th Street. Once you do find it, though, you'll see that it's full of merchandise wherever you turn. It's better than most thrifts of this type because of the vintage clothes plus a few well-known designer labels mixed in with everything else.

This place is also great for people looking for merchandise with pictures of pets on them, like dogs or cats on china or mugs. They're often donated by pet owners who already have too many cat plates, or can't get their dog to climb those doggie steps someone bought them for Christmas. Best of all, every dime you spend here supports a wonderful no-kill not-for-profit pet shelter that serves southeast Florida: Tri-County Animal Rescue.

VINTAGE HOME COLLECTIVE

www.vintagehomecollective.com; Facebook: Vintage Home
Collective // 141 W. 20th St., Suite H3 / Boca Raton 33431 / (561)
510-0842 / OPEN: Tues.-Sat. 10:30-4

It's strange to find a high-end home accent shop in a mall whose
main attraction is their two large thrift shops: LEVIS JCC and
HOSPICE BY THE SEA CHEST. But almost hidden at the end of
the square are a collection of small women-owned shops, all offering
interesting merchandise that may seem a bit expensive if you've just
visited the two thrifts.

Originally, this storefront just held Laura's PAPILLON VINTAGE
HOME shop, where you could—and still can—find great décor,
vintage items, "upcycled elegance" and redone furniture. Now,
VINTAGE MIDCENTURY, HENAO GLASS and BAY 38 have
come aboard and also occupy this expanded area. All the areas
contain a variety of work by talented artists and designers. They also
have classes in furniture painting, jewelry making, glass making and
seasonal home décor. But go here *before* you hit the two nearby
thrifts at this mall so the prices will seem more reasonable.

೮ාೞ
BARGAIN SAVING TIP

If you want better clothes, go to a consignment shop. If you
want better bargains, go to a thrift shop. (See Part IV)
People bring clothes good enough to sell to a consignment
shop and receive a percentage of what the store obtains,
usually 50%. People give away clothes to thrift shops, so
generally they're not as good as what they could consign for
money. But a "quality thrift" accepts free donations, but are
choosy about what they sell, so they generally carry better
merchandise .

೮ාೞ

Delray Beach

A BLAST FROM THE PAST

www.facebook.com/ablastfromthepastdelray // 777 E. Atlantic Ave. / Delray Beach 33483 / (561) 272-8290 / OPEN: Mon.-Fri. 12:30-8; Sat. 12:30-9:30; Sun. 12:30-8

Much is unique and often very rare here. You'll find original Puccis. Guccis. Hermes. Miriam Haskell jewelry. Perfect condition handbags. A lot of it is vintage, but some of the merchandise is new. And what's also unusual is they've sold contemporary bags, like Chanels, at the same time as vintage Chanels. The prices are high, but not for what you're getting.

The layout is simple and there's a lot of room to browse. There's also an adjoining shop in the back of the adjacent via that carries jewelry and collectibles. Dee will be glad to help you, and tell you about how she used to determine the price by the roll of the dice. She had a fuzzy die, and when you checked out, she tossed it. Depending on whether it landed on 5, 10, or 15, that was the percentage off that you received.

A UNIQUE VINTAGE CONSIGNMENT BOUTIQUE

Facebook: A Unique Vintage Consignment Boutique // 15119 Jog Rd. / Delray Beach 33446 / (561) 270-2945 / OPEN: Tues.-Sat. "11ish-5ish," they say.

Despite its slightly cumbersome name, this is a great vintage boutique. This three-year-old one-room emporium is run by a mother and daughter who carry clothes from every era at a surprisingly low cost. "We're not crazy with our prices," said Audrey. Happily, that's true. For example, a fluffy gray fur fox stole that would have gone for hundreds in Palm Beach was only $75.

Audrey explained that there were many communities in the area (like Kings Point) with older residents who go through their closets and bring in their parents' and even grandparents' clothes to them. This also explains the dozens of brooches pinned to a mannequin, just one example of the creativity evidenced here.

They also carry some vintage wedding dresses, like the custom made Chloe gown from the 1940's for $125 that was there when I was visiting. So were a lot of one-of-a-kind garments and accessories you won't find elsewhere and definitely at that price. They also have a few more modern home décor items sprinkled around.

BETHESDA BARGAIN BOX

www.bethesdaweb.com/bethesda-bargain-box; Facebook: Bethesda Bargain Box // 12 NE 5th Ave. (southbound Federal Hwy.) / Delray Beach 33483 / (561) 278-2401 / OPEN: Mon.-Fri. 10-5; Sat. 10-2

"Bargain Box" is an apt name for this popular Delray thrift, although the word "box" might lead you to believe that it's small, Bethesda Bargain Box definitely is not. It's one of the largest thrifts between Boca Raton and Jupiter, and there are many different sections to explore in this "box."

The large main room, filled with boutique clothes, shoes, lingerie, children's toys, glassware and home décor is worth the trip alone. Especially since the prices are so good they could best be described as double take, particularly when there's a sale of some sort, which frequently occurs.

Continue on through a winding alleyway of photo frames, art, books (probably the largest collection of books outside of a real library) until you reach "The Barn." It's filled with lower-end bric-a-brac and linens, and mostly not-so-new furniture, but at sensational prices, especially the outdoor furniture. To top it off, in the corner, they also have golf clubs for $3-$5, and golf shoes for $5-$9.

This shop has been in existence since 1962 and is expertly managed by Michelle Esposito, and her Mom is often at the counter. Michelle says they offer "boutique-style shopping where everything is sized and organized for you." She's right.

SHOP NEARBY: An outlet jewelry shop, SEQUIN DELRAY BEACH at 445 E. Atlantic. Stunning stuff! And affordable!

NOTE: Parking for Bethesda (and Sequin): Going south on NE 5th Avenue, keep an eye open for a small parking lot on the right before the store. It says "Bethesda Bargain Box" on the wall.

BIG APPLE SHOPPING BAZAAR

www.thebigappleshoppingbazaar.com; www.facebook.com
/DelrayFlea Market // 5283 W. Atlantic Ave. / Delray Beach 33484 /
(561) 499-9935 / OPEN: Wed.-Sat. 10-5:30; Sun. 11-5

I really can't recommend this place. So many of the booths appear to
be closed or unmanned (unwomaned?) which is depressing, and
several of the rest carry mostly the same stuff booth after booth,
especially glasses, and cosmetics. Yes, there are a few unique
shops—the best is the pickle guy *outside* of the mall — offering
specialized services or whatever. And a friend told me she liked their
wig booth, which is the first I knew that she was wearing one so it
must be good. But in general, this place is hardly worth going to.

Still, if you insist, what you'll find will definitely be cheaper than in a
regular store. But you'll use up your savings on the gas to get there.
Better still, use up *more* gas and go to FESTIVAL (SAMPLE
ROAD) FLEA MARKET. (See Part 2, Broward/Miami chapter.) It's
not great but it's a lot better than this.

FRUGAL FASHIONISTA

www.frugalfashionstashop.com; www.Facebook: Frugal Fashionista
Resale Boutique // 825 N. Federal Hwy., (or NE 6th Ave) / Delray
Beach 33435 / (561) 865-7857 / OPEN: Tues.-Sat. 11-5

One block north of George Bush Boulevard
is a resale shop where the owner, Amber
Ortoll, sells a lovely assortment of stylish
women's clothes at prices that will wow you.
What will you find there? "I'm a style
schizophrenic because I like a lot of things,"
Amber admitted.

The varied offerings—she calls them "re-
chic boutique" are all very attractive and
extremely well priced, perfect for those who
are "frugal" and want to be "fashionistas," just as the store name
promises.

Almost nothing is more than $30 and a lot is less than that. For
example, a pair of Stuart Weitzman shoes in good condition went for

$20. An unworn Ralph Lauren blouse was in the $20 area. There are also fun hats and shoes and a closet full of Lily Pulitzers as well. Bottom line: the clothes are smart, many of the labels will be known to you, and everything is sold for a lot less than what you'd pay at other consignments. Plus, you can usually find a discount rack by the register.

GREAT STUFF PREVIOUSLY ENJOYED
901 George Bush Blvd. / Delray Beach 33483 / (561) 243-0010 / OPEN: Mon.-Sat. 10-4:30

There's not much of what you would call a bargain in this upscale home décor and art consignment shop west of the Intercostal. There are a few small items for under $25 but that's not why you would come here. You should pay them a visit just to wander through the unusual and beautiful home décor which looks like it just came out of a retail shop—or "Architectural Digest." You'll be "oohing"  and "aahing" as you walk through their two large rooms and alleys to view the six sections filled with wonderful home accents and furniture. Although it's not that large, it's easy to get lost when trying to leave because you have to work your way back to the only entrance. But what a wonderful place to get "lost" in!

GUTSY BOUTIQUE
Facebook: Gutsy Boutique // 13800 Jog Rd. / Delray Beach 33446 / (561) 364-4888 / OPEN: Mon.-Sat. 10-5

This is in the San Marco Shops in the western part of Delray Beach. It's similar to another not-too-far-away women's consignment, MONA LISA, but this is the slightly larger of the two. Both carry a small amount of new as well as consigned clothes, with separate racks for petites, Chicos, and clearance.

Gutsy doesn't divide the new from the resale, which is a bit confusing. Reductions are also haphazard. "Periodically I'll run around and mark things off," says the owner, Rochelle Love. *Note:* You can buy a T-shirt here saying "Gutsy," if you want to advertise the store—or your spirit.

GUTSY GOWNS

A few doors down in the same mall is Gutsy's second shop, carrying formal, cocktail and special occasion clothes, "fancy shoes, fancy handbags, and fancy jewelry." Fancy that!

This small shop, open only from 11-4, is stocked with everything for going out on special occasions. That includes wedding dresses, mother-of-the-bride ones, bridesmaid gowns, and more. "We're not Chanel," said the salesperson. "Someone can buy a lovely gown here for under $200."

There was an interesting story behind the most expensive gown there during my first check of the place. It was a $429 spectacular-looking silk organza wedding dress with a beaded satin bodice and matching beaded jacket that originally cost $8,000. The owner had never worn it. When she consigned it here, she commented that the gown cost her a lot less money than the marriage would have cost her had she gone through it. (Facebook: Gutsy Gowns)

KISMET OF DELRAY

www.kismetvintage.com; Facebook: Kismet Vintage // Pineapple Grove Arts District, 157 NE 2nd Ave. / Delray Beach 33444 / (561) 865-7895 / OPEN: Mon.-Fri. 11-6; Sat. 10-8; Sun. 11-4

This vintage and designer clothing shop off the main street in Delray's Atlantic Avenue trades clothes, giving you 40% on the spot for what you bring in that they accept. While trading clothes here may be nice, shopping may be even more rewarding. You can find good recycled eco-friendly clothing in this relatively uncluttered place owned by husband and wife, Aly and Lee Sutherland. Besides vintage labels you may or may not have heard of, they feature some current designer labels you may know. For example, they had a man's Robert Graham shirt (normally in the $200+ area) for $60. An even more expensive Etro men's shirt was one-third less than at Neiman Marcus.

NOTE: This shop is next to the famous **Max's Harvest Restaurant**.

MIMI'S CHEST

mimischest.weebly.com; Facebook: Mimis Chest // 400 Gulfstream Blvd. / Delray Beach 33444 / (561)271-3937/ OPEN: Tues-Sun 11-5:30

This "gift shop with furniture"—as owner Mimi Rizek refers to it—isn't a thrift or consignment shop. What do you call a fabulous little house, overflowing with the most marvelously fun décor and gifts that she has purchased and is now selling at a low, low price? A great find.

I lost count of how many small rooms and alcoves there are—I think 11 including 3 bathrooms, and what's in there is for sale too so that counts. To find it (a bit difficult the first time, but you will be back), turn at the Dunkin' Donuts on Federal, and on Gulfstream Boulevard. Go about a block and you'll see the little house on the left. *Voilá!* (Note to pet lovers: there are many wonderful dog and cat items here.)

SHOP NEARBY: WALMART at 3627 Federal Highway.

MONA LISA FASHIONS, INC.

www.monalisafashions.com; www.facebook.com/MonaLisaFashionsInc, and www.ebay.com/usr/monalisafashionsboutique // 7431 W. Atlantic Ave., Suite 50 / Delray Beach 33446 / (561) 865-2541 / OPEN: Mon.-Sat. 10-5; Sun. (mid-November to mid-April) 12-4:30

The Village of Oriole Shops is best-known for a large kosher supermarket named Glicks. At the other end of the mall, though, you'll find Mona Lisa, whose motto is: "An Affordable Way to Look Fashionable."

A few things stand out from many other consignment shops like this. There's a Chico rack, a rack of petites, and two racks of samples, which Mona Lisa (yes, that is her first and middle name) sells at cost to lure people in.

The jewelry was unimpressive and there were no knockouts (or knock-offs) among the handbags. But pop in and you might pop out with something.

SHOP NEARBY: There's an interesting shop next door at Suite 51 called **REVA'S HANDBAGS & ACCESSORIES**. This tiny place carries mid-range handbags, gift items, tote bags, backpacks, makeup cases, travel cases and you name it. Some of it is 50-70% less than at most retail outlets, and they even recently had a $200 bag which they were selling for $20. If you're in the neighborhood for Glicks, or Mona Lisa's, definitely stop by. As they say in this mall, it wouldn't hurt. (561) 381-4777.

NEST

www.nestdelray.com; www.facebook.com/NestOfdelray // 817 NE 6th Ave. /Delray Beach 33483 /(561)900-7181 / OPEN: Mon.-Sat. 10:30-5

If you really like country beachy stuff, and as their ad says "trendy vintage furniture & home décor," you might want to stop at this small shop—you can't miss it with all the furniture outside—especially if you're next door at the wonderful **FRUGAL FASHIONISTA**.

Unfortunately, the parking for Nest is grim. There are a couple of spaces slightly north of the shop, but then you have to back your car into heavy traffic to get out.... nothing here is worth an accident.

They carry vintage, (no clothes, tiny amount of jewelry), along with refinished and custom furniture and home décor. Often some good pillows. You can get a feel for what's here by going to their website or Facebook page (see above) but the items look a lot better there. Besides, it's a lot easier "getting around" online than in this small cluttered shop—and you don't have to park!

RESTORE (HABITAT FOR HUMANITY)

www.habitat.org/restores // 1900 N. Federal Hwy. / Delray Beach 33483 / (561) 455-4441/ OPEN: Tues.-Sat. 10-6; Sun. 11-5

This is one of a well-known group of thrift shops for people looking for furniture, home appliances, and specific items for home building (such as doors, sconces, hurricane shutters, decorator items, and household construction pieces) without paying a lot of money for them.

But household goods aren't all they have there. They're so diverse that they even carry Christmas-related merchandise all year round. Indeed, this ReStore shop is like Christmas in July because it's such a gift to find a huge well-lit store with shockingly low prices and a lot of really nice necessities as well as serendipitous ones you don't need. (But what the heck—at those prices, buy them anyway.) That includes not only excellent furniture at thrift store prices but a small selection of clothes, books, paintings, and gifts. But don't expect glamor here. "It's like a clean Goodwill with furniture," said one customer.

OTHER RESTORE/HABITAT FOR HUMANITY SHOPS:

272 S. Dixie Hwy. / Boca Raton 33432 / (561) 362-7284 // 34639 Lake Worth Rd. / Greenacres 33463 / (561) 202-1630 // 1635 N. Old Dixie Hwy. / Jupiter 33469 / (561) 743-3660 (See Jupiter/Juno chapter) // 26831 N. Military Trail / West Palm Beach 33407 / (561) 253-2290

SECOND TIME AROUND

www.2tadelray.com; Facebook: Second Time Around Women's Apparel // 801 George Bush Blvd. / Delray Beach 33483 / (561) 278-0493 / OPEN: Mon.-Sun. 10-5

Second Time Around has been around since 1980, when it acquired a legion of dedicated followers at their SE 4th Street site. Now it really is the second time around for them because they've moved to George Bush Boulevard, off Federal.

There's always a rack of heavily reduced clothes outside, and the prices inside the shop are good too. Although it's small, you'll find casual, professional, and evening clothes along with a smattering of shoes, handbags and a lot of costume jewelry here.

SNAPPY TURTLE OUTLETS

www.snappy-turtle.com // 2512 N. Federal Hwy. / Delray Beach / (561) 276-3308 / OPEN: Mon.-Sat. 10-5

At 2512 N. Federal Highway in a large room are the same great deals as the regular store at least 50% and often even less on what they stock at the main store (which is about 15 minutes away), namely, women's clothes, some men's, and children's, and a smattering of home interior products as well.

RESTAURANT NEARBY: At **ELLIE'S 50'S DINER**, you can find a bit of neon nostalgia with waitresses wearing pink poodle skirts, and menu items named for the 50's. Hearing so much Elvis from their jukebox can leave you all shook up, but, hey, that's when your heartache begins. 2410 N. Federal Hwy. (561 276-1570) Cash only.

TRUE TREASURES DELRAY BEACH

www.truetreasuresinc.com // Military & Atlantic next to Winn Dixie / Delray Beach 33484 / (561) 699-9797/OPEN: Mon.-Sat. 10-8; Sun. 11-6

Southern Palm Beach County now can enjoy what Northern Palm Beach County has loved for over 25 years in two locations. (See Lake Park/North Palm Beach and Palm Beach Gardens chapters.)

At 14,000 square feet, True Treasure's latest store has the finest furnishing coming from spectacular homes in Palm Beach County all the way down to Miami. This Delray newcomer has many décor items and shipments are received daily. Their motto: "Why Pay Retail when you can find a True Treasure?"

ଛଠଔ

AFFORDABLE ART

Where can you buy original art these days? So few galleries are left that an increasing number of artists are bringing their work into consignment shops to sell their paintings. Owners are also bringing them into these places if they want to make some money or are redecorating. So, if you're looking for paintings, start looking at the walls of the furnishings and home décor shops that you visit.

ଛଠ ଔ

JACK THE RIPPER
IN DELRAY BEACH

Driving toward the ocean on Atlantic, you'll find an interesting restaurant with a connection to Jack the Ripper and Winston Churchill. And the food is great as well!

The Blue Anchor British Pub was an authentic 1864 Anglican drinking establishment that was dismantled and shipped piece-by-piece across the ocean to its current spot at 804 Atlantic Ave.

During its earlier incarnation, when it was on famed Chancery Lane in London, two of its patrons were ultimately victims of the Ripper. A third loyal customer (but obviously not at the same time) was Winston Churchill.

Another regular was a woman murdered in the pub by her jealous husband. It is said by some that her ghost continues to haunt the halls of the Blue Anchor. If so, it may be the first ghost to ever cross the Atlantic.

෨෨

DECORATING IN DELRAY

There are several interesting shops—four are next to each other—along a strip on Federal Highway. They range from tiny to gargantuan, and if you're looking for home décor, collectibles, and furnishings ranging from modern to vintage, it's worth stopping by these stores, listed alphabetically below.

DECORATOR ROW

1550 N. Federal Hwy. / Delray Beach / (561) 303-1456 & (561) 278-5999 / OPEN: Mon.-Sun. 10-7

This small easy-to-miss mall (it's between the large RESTORE thrift shop and a spa) consists of several small home décor shops so filled you can hardly get around a few of them. But if you're looking for used, vintage and consignment home décor at a really good price and you don't care about atmosphere, don't miss the very sudden turnoff into this mall.

If you don't accidentally pass it by, you'll find everything here from small furniture to jewelry, lighting, antiques, art, home décor, china, and collectibles. Their already low prices are often even lower since they're open to negotiation.

The names of the places seem to keep changing, along with the owners, but currently there's BEACHED IN DELRAY, BLISS (old and new furniture), MARG OF PEPPER PIKE (unusual hand-made jewelry, see margofpepperpike.com), and the best of them all, Elaine's THEN AND NOW CONSIGNMENT where you're sure to find something unique and priced to move and you'll want to make it part of your home.

EAST COAST FURNITURE

www.eastcoastfurniture.net; Facebook: East Coast Furniture Co // 1319 N. Federal Hwy. / Delray Beach / (561) 265-3749 / OPEN: Mon.-Sat. 9-6; Sun. 12-5.

There's a surprise here and it's not *in* the shop but in back of it. There you'll find a large outdoor patio section with tons of chairs, chaises, and tables. Indoors, well, it's filled with traditional wooden furniture giving it a dark and unexciting look. You can get an idea of what it's like by looking at the photo on their website.

If you get past that uninviting first room, in the second one there are a few attractive pieces at good prices, e.g., a stunning lamp that was $150 at a northern furniture consignment was $89 there. They also offer good deals on new bedding.

East Coast has been run by the same family for over 50 years, and they have a similar shop in Lantana at 6092 South Congress Avenue called FURNITURE DISCOVERY Inc. (561) 434-4200. Over on the west side of the county, you'll find FURNITURE ADVENTURE at 5301 State Road 7 (Highway 441) in Lake Worth (561) 766-1609.

ELRAY FURNITURE

www.Elrayofdelray.com; Facebook: Elray of Delray Furniture // 2004 N. Federal Hwy. / Delray Beach / (561) 272-5995 / OPEN: Tues.-Fri. 10-6; Sat. 10-5; Sun 10-5

This is another one of these places where you might think that the junky looking furniture outside is a reflection of what you'll find inside. That's why I've never dropped by. But when I finally did, I found a lot of attractive pieces along with some really unusual ones. Like the deer's head, and the wild boar's head, perhaps to end up above the fireplace of a sly purchaser who wants to convince people that he hunted for more than just bargains.

The price point for everything there was nothing to write home about, but if you're looking for mid-century modern, Florida "vintage" Faux Bamboo & Rattan, Lucite Furnishings, lots of coffee tables and accessories you should pay them a visit.

GRANDPA'S ATTIC

www.grandpasattic.biz // 7720 N. Federal Hwy. / Delray Beach / (561) 571-7337 / OPEN: Mon.-Sat. 10-5

You would expect a place that included the name "Grandpa's" to be filled with fusty and dusty old furniture. So imagine my surprise to discover that this stand-alone building had the largest collection of modern mirrored furniture (dressers, tables, accents etc.,) that I've seen anyplace.

Besides the pre-owned and new furniture, all in perfect condition, and at good prices, I was delighted to find one of the largest collection of costume jewelry from the 1920's to today that I've seen anyplace. And the price point was *excellent.*

The owner claimed there were over a thousand pieces there, and what I especially liked was that I could easily see the (low) prices clearly even though the jewelry was kept behind large glass cabinets.

Indeed, one of those cabinets contained only Bakelite jewelry, a collector's delight for those into what passed for funk in the '20's and '30's. (TIP: Although the Bakelite here is real, there's a lot of "Fakelite" around. The say the trick for telling if it's real is to place the jewelry in hot water, then remove and sniff. Warmed Bakelite smells like camphor.)

Don't pass this place by if you love costume jewelry and glittery furniture!

Jupiter, Juno Beach & Tequesta

A STAR'S CLOSET

www.astarscloset.com; Facebook: A Stars Closet // Concourse
Village / 75 E. Indiantown Rd., #503 / Jupiter 33477 / (561) 747-
0240 / OPEN: Mon.-Fri. 10-5:30; Sat. 10-5

A stylish upscale consignment shop with cutting edge clothes, and to
top it off, it's located in an easy-to-find mall. Claudette Cerro, the
owner for over 23 years (she also works with her sister, Line), has
filled her shop with trendy accessories and attractive designer
women's apparel, such as colorful Lilly Pulitzer and classic St. John
knits.

In addition, the two showcases of unique jewelry, both vintage and
new, had many attractive pieces in them. Put this on your must-try-
out list and it will become one of your regular haunts.

CLASSIC FURNISHINGS

www.classicfurnishingsoftequesta.com; Facebook: Classic
Furnishings Tequesta Florida // Village Square Mall, 161 N. U.S.
Hwy.1 / Tequesta 33469 / (561) 575-7107 / OPEN: Mon.-Sun. 9-5

Don't go looking in the old location (223 S. US Hwy. 1) for this shop
because it's moved nearby to the Home Goods/Marshall Plaza. But do
look for it if you want to buy patio furniture with the
Florida/Bahamas wicker rattan-tropical look.

Even so, there's much more here than just that. They're one of the
largest furniture consignment stores in Palm Beach County. This
family-owned store, which has been in the business for over 30 years,
has everything—and in mint condition. They also sell regular retail.

If you're a decorator or realtor, this may also be the place for you
since they're one of the few furniture resalers offering a buy-back
guarantee for model rooms. They promise to repurchase (at 50%
minus sales tax) what you paid for the furniture when you return it.
(But you may fall in love with it and be unable to part with it.)

***SHOP NEARBY:* A WHITE PENGUIN** is a quaint "consignment

nook" as the owners, Mary Ellen and Jim White describe it. They sell some unusual home furnishings, décor, accessories, and artwork, and offer a wide variety of antique and modern furniture and home accents. It's at Gallery Square North, 387 Tequesta Drive / Tequesta / (561) 972-4791 / OPEN Mon.-Fri. 10-4; Sat. 10-3.

CONSIGN-IT JUPITER

Facebook: Consign-it-Jupiter // 615 W. Indiantown Rd., Ste. 107 / Jupiter 33458 / (561) 972-4084 / OPEN: Mon.-Sat. 9-5

This furniture emporium in the Big Dollar Plaza across from Wendy's doesn't just carry furniture, home goods, and jewelry. They carry *interesting* furnishings, home décor, and jewelry. You'll see many different mixes of style, sizes (including larger pieces) all extremely well priced. The friendly staff—it's family run—immediately approaches you to help find what you want, which isn't difficult here.

To give you an idea of what I and others found, I was amazed to see a double outdoor chaise, which is hard to find new, and then it costs around $2000-$4,000. Here, it was $600 and in excellent condition. The *Examiner's* frugal living blogger, Nancy Munro, stumbled upon an even hard-to-find trundle bed. She reported finding everything from a $4 miniature brass pitcher to a $4,000 chandelier. When I was there they had neither, but they had a number of display cabinets, "from an antique curio to units large enough for your HDTV." There's also a Waterford crystal collection and not just boring glasses "but everything from a honey pot to a golf trophy." New items arrive Tuesday and Thursday and there are customers waiting…. Not surprising. *SHOP NEARBY*: Next door is **FURRY FRIENDS THRIFT SHOP**. (See Section IV for Thrift shops.)

ುೆ

"When women are depressed, they eat or go shopping. Men invade another country. It's a whole different way of thinking."

—Elayne Boosler

FOREVER YOUNG CHILDREN'S CONSIGNMENT INC.

Facebook: Forever Young Children's Consignment Inc. // Fashion Mall, 150 N. U.S.1, Suite 7/ Tequesta 33469 / (561)746-3776 OPEN: Tue.-Fri. 10-5; Sat. 10-4

Two "Kims," Kim Choynowski and Kim Robbins, own this large, bright, and cheerful boutique which opened in January 2009. It carries gently used children's clothing from newborn to size 8, maternity clothing, nursery furniture & equipment, toys, books, DVD's, new dancewear, infant and toddler swimwear, and new baby gift items. BONUS: There's a special area for children to play in while their parents are shopping.

HABITAT FOR HUMANITY

www.palmbeach.habitatrestores.org//1635 N. Old Dixie Hwy / Jupiter 33469 / (561)743-3660 / OPEN: Mon.-Wed. 9-4; Thurs. 9-5; Fri. Sat. 9-4

There are several Habitat for Humanity Thrift Shops (See Boca chapter) but they're not anything like this one. In fact, few thrift shops are like this one. It's in a stand-alone building and it's humongous. Indeed, as you walk around you find more and more rooms.

The best is the back one, the Boutique. Most thrift shop "boutiques" may have a few worthwhile garments, but this really was a boutique with a lot of better offerings. Up front is also good with more expensive items but still well priced: a Tiffany key holder with the box was $95; a largish cute Swarovski Dalmatian dog was $88; a gorgeous blue Kosta Boda bowl was $20. This front room holds the better gifts and decorative pieces in a couple of glass cases along with some forgettable jewelry. On the other side are several large couches and pieces of furniture priced so low as to be almost ridiculous. Make this one your favorite Habitats; make it one of your favorite thrift shops.

HOSPICE: RESALE SHOP NORTH

www.hpbc.com/resale // Plaza La Mer, 863 Donald Ross Rd. / Juno Beach 33408 / (561) 624-5495 / OPEN: Mon.-Sat. 10-5

A lot of good merchandise is ready to leave here and find a home—yours—in this spacious, cheerful, five-room thrift shop. You could easily buy something from any section. That's especially true of the two ample-sized rooms of furniture, which feature particularly attractive unused-looking couches, chairs, and tables. The men and women's clothing sections have some occasional finds and are mostly what you'd find in a typical (or inexpensive) consignment shop, but with cheaper prices.

NOTE: In back of the counter are some additional better items but they're often overpriced. Same for the two upright glass cases at the entrance.

CONSIGNMENT SHOP NEARBY: **LADIES CLOSET** at 849 Donald Ross Road is in the same mall a few doors over.

JUPITER MEDICAL CENTER THRIFT SHOP

www.jupitermed.com/thrift-shop// 205 Center St./ Jupiter 33458/(561) 746-1601 / OPEN: Mon.-Fri. 9:30-4; Sat. 9-2

Toward the back of the Jupiter Medical Center Thrift Shop was a rack of St. Johns. Wait a minute? St. John in a thrift shop? Well, many pleasant surprises await you here. In addition to the typical thrift goods, they also sell musical instruments, cars, and even boats.

This unusually large, clean thrift is definitely worth a visit because of its great prices for attractive clothes, decorative accessories (especially those in the glass cases), and household goods. There's also a large men's section to the left.

DON'T MISS: If you look straight ahead, you'll see what appears to be a room of books. But when you enter it, you'll encounter a large area to the right containing mainly household goods and goodies.

LADIES CLOSET

48 Donald Ross Rd. / Juno Beach 33408 / (561) 223-2623 / OPEN: Tues.-Sat. 10-5

This is run by a mother and daughter who have put together a medium-sized, pleasant women's consignment shop where you can walk comfortably admiring the high-end—and affordable—very attractive, almost new-looking designer merchandise. A trip to Ladies Closet and to the excellent HOSPICE thrift shop, which is just a few doors away, is almost reason enough to make a trip to this mall. And if you're a cat lover, you'll want to go the cat thrift as well.

MAN CAVE

www.mancaveconsign.com; Facebook: Man Cave Consignments // 1535 Cypress Dr., Unit 2 / Jupiter 33469 / (561) 746-2283 / OPEN: Tues.-Fri. 10-5; Sat. 10-2

Fortunately, this doesn't look like a man cave, which one might expect to be dark, dirty and messy. Instead, this is a small bright shop featuring the too-often neglected area of men's better clothing, carrying (at considerably reduced prices) everything from jeans to evening wear, from low prices to well.....

But a man can find more than just clothes here. The Man Cave also carries sporting equipment, memorabilia (sports pictures, posters, etc.,) electronics (pretested to make sure they work), tools, stuff for garages, boats, jukeboxes, recliners, and more of what guys like.

They promise a "relaxed, fun and comfortable place where guys can go to be guys and shop for things that guys love." And they also cater to the cave woman searching for the right item for her cave man. So both sexes can feel very comfortable shopping here.

PENNIES FOR HEAVEN THRIFT SHOP

www.goodsheponline.org/thrift-shop.html; Facebook: Pennies for Heaven Thrift Shop //Church of the Good Shepherd, 400 Seabrook Rd. /Tequesta 33469 / (561)746-4674x112/ OPEN: Tues.-Fri. 9-4; Sat. 10-2

This thrift and boutique with the clever name belongs to the Episcopal Church of the Good Shepherd, and it's one of the oldest thrifts in the county. It has been around for 40 years and is located just off the courtyard on the church grounds. Volunteers and shoppers sometimes call this "Tequesta's best kept secret" because of the merchandise and prices.

They carry mostly women's clothing and accessories, although they have some select garments for children, and men. On one recent inspection, a nice sports coat was selling for $7.50—fully lined.

TEQUESTA STOCK EXCHANGE

www.tequestastockexchangeinc.com; Facebook: Tequesta Stock Exchange Inc // Tequesta Fashion Mall, 150 U.S.1, Ste. 19 / Tequesta 33469 / (561) 746-0046 / OPEN: Tues.-Sat. 10-5

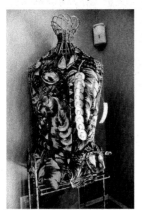

The name "stock exchange" is a clever one for a ladies consignment shop, but the real "stock exchange" is a place where you might lose something, namely your money. This stock exchange is one in which you have to come out ahead if you buy something because everything is great and the prices are more than right. No wonder it was voted Number 1 in Women's Consignment shops!

It's one of the best-known best-liked consignment shops in the area, and it's certainly one of my favorite in the whole northern part of the county. This bright attractive shop isn't that large, but its range of women's clothes is and the selection is exciting. I don't know how they get so much great merchandise in here without it feeling crowded but they do. The charming owner, Linda O'Loughlin, is another reason people come here. Even when other shops are empty (and the owners complaining), people just seem to be keep arriving.

THE GOOD STUFF

www.thegoodstuffconsignment.com & Facebook: The Good Stuff //
129 Center St. / Jupiter 33469 / (561) 746-8004 / OPEN: Mon. 10-5;
Tues.-Fri. 10-6; Sat. 10-5; Sun. 10-2

Remember the good old days when The Good Stuff was a funky shop
in a charming cottage with a purple awning and three wild and crazy
gals stocked three rooms of offbeat home decor at fabulous prices?

Plus, if you came in on a Tuesday wearing a tiara they would give
you a discount! Of course, the girls who owned the shop were
sporting their tiaras on Tuesday—as were plenty of men who came
there to shop on Tiara Tuesdays as well!

Well, things change. The girls sold The Good Stuff and it moved, and
it's just one large room now, which is heavy on cottage
coastal/beachy/shabby chic—and the prices are not what they once
were. But at least they still have Tiara Tuesday.

.

ഇന്ദ്ര
WHERE TOM CRUISED...

How do people feel about buying clothes worn by celebrities? Not
only do they want them, but the great unwashed wants the great,
unwashed. Meaning that the average person wants clothes that
famous people have worn without being laundered or anything of
the celebrity taken away.

"People want them dirty lest Brad Pitt or Barack Obama's fairy dust
fall(s) off," says Paul Bloom, the author of "How Pleasure Works."

If they want this "aura" on the clothes (or in Tom Cruise's case, the
body thetans or alien beings he has paid millions to Scientology to
try to eradicate), how do people feel about wearing clothes that have
been worn by killers? Ewwww. People who were told that a sweater
was worn by a murderer said they wouldn't wear it.

ഇന്ദ്ര

Lake Park & North Palm Beach

COASTAL MARKET PLACE

Facebook: Coastal Market Place // 216 N. Federal Hwy. / Lake Park 33403 / (561) 460-1071 / OPEN: Mon.-Thurs. 10-5; Fri. Sat. 10-6; Sun. 12-5

Coastal Marketplace is home to a unique array of imaginative items with a nautical theme. Their motto is "Love where you Live!" So live it up and you'll love it here.

They're located on US 1 across from the oldest Dunkin Donuts in Lake Park. Once there, you'll encounter an array of unexpected finds. Another nice touch: their collaboration with local Coastal Artists. They also up-cycle one-of-a-kind furniture pieces. Custom pieces can be quoted for free. Whatever you'll find, it will be one-of-a-kind, as is this shop.

SHOP NEARBY: Right next door is **ST. MARK'S THRIFT SHOP**. (See Part IV on Thrift Shops)

CONSIGNED COUTURE

www.facebook.com/consigned.couture.9 // 524 Northlake Blvd. / Lake Park 33408 / (561) 881-9005 / OPEN: Mon.-Sat. 11-6

This shop has moved from 932 Northlake into a small mall making it a bit harder to find. It's also expanded to such a degree that it may now be the largest clothing consignment shop in the county.

They've also added a large line of men's clothes.

Not to mention their handbags: Purses are propped, perched and hanging everywhere, leaning against the walls, and sitting patiently in back of the counter. In the glass showcases, they also display an attractive selection of jewelry.

The clothes in Elizabeth Araujo's crowded shop are good too—some are even geared toward a younger crowd—making browsing a wonderful adventure.

CONSIGNMENT WAREHOUSE

Facebook: Vals Red Hat Consignment Shop//1183 Old Dixie Hwy./ Lake Park 33403/ (561) 568-8257 / OPEN: Mon.-Fri 10-5; Sat. 10-whenever.

Are you in for a surprise when you enter this place! Outside Consignment Warehouse, formerly Val's Red Hat, it looks like an optical shop with two large iconic Shepherd's glasses. But inside... wow! Five thousand-square-feet of everything you could possibly want and so much is unique and delightful. You probably wouldn't have bought the real musk that was once there for $2,500, but you'll find something else there now and for a lot less. And what fun it is to walk from room to room, alcove to alcove. And if you don't find what you're looking for, ask Val, because she keeps even more unusual fare in their storage units.

People come from miles around—from Singer Island, Ibis, Palm Beach and North Palm Beach for the unusual vintage and modern and in-betweens. There are even some clothes in a large alcove filled with "After 5's." but there's so much than just that here.

Even the owner, Val, is more than a shop owner: she's a licensed optician, a licensed massage therapist, and a licensed real estate broker. "This is another hat I wear," she says.

DECORATORS RESOURCE

www.decoratorsresourcepalmbeach.com; Facebook: Decorators Resource Estate Furnishings // 333 US Hwy.1 / Lake Park 33403 / (561) 845-9648 / OPEN: Mon.—Sat. 9:30-5:30; Sun. 12 - 5

If you're decorating a home—or you're a designer or dealer—you should know about this humongous (10,000 square feet) high-end furniture store. At 10,000 square feet with a dozen alcoves, it's one of the largest furniture emporiums in the county. Some of it is consigned, some of it is estate, but if you're decorating a home—or you're a designer or dealer—you should definitely come to this high-end furniture store. This place has it all, from kitchen, patio, garden, and barware accessories to dining, seating and garden furniture, lighting and home décor items. They've been around for 20 years, always a good sign.

If you're looking for bargains, go to their website, and on the upper right hand corner of the front page, sign up for their special discounts.

DEJA NEW GALLERY
www.facebook.com/DejaNewGallery // 212 US Hwy. 1 / North Palm Beach 33408 / (561) 844-1151/ OPEN: Mon. Sat. 10-6; Sun. 11- 4

Because of its name, you might confuse this place near Lake Park for Déjà Vu, the large estate liquidator shops in PBG. Or you might erroneously think this is an art gallery, and there you would be closer to the truth because they do have a lot of interesting art here. Also, unusual lighting, from dramatic pole lamps to exotic chandeliers. And when you stop looking up at the chandeliers and look down, you'll see lots of colorful carpeting, including outdoor carpets, which are so popular they can barely keep them in stock.

But there's a lot more in this gallery than just art, carpeting, and lighting. It's so chock-full that you can hardly get around. And when you do, you'll find an incredibly eclectic assortment of everything from a new Japanese side table to floral lamp shades to framed New Yorker covers. Says co-owner Amanda: "If you like it, we'll discount down." The prices are so good, you may not even bothering asking.

PALM BEACH REGENCY
www.Palmbeachregency.com; Facebook: Palm Beach Regency // 850 Old Dixie Hwy./Lake Park / (561) 252-7381 / OPEN: Tues.-Sat. 10-4

They sell mostly to designers and dealers at this vintage furniture boutique, but if you're looking for Old Florida-Palm Beach style from the '70s, you'll find plenty of it here. Actually, if you're looking for any kind of vintage furniture you should pay a visit to this 5,000-square-foot "furniture boutique," which also has an adjoining 1,000 feet of additional warehouse space.

You'll find lots of chairs, cabinets, étagères, screens, mirrors, lighting, (lamps & chandeliers), headboards, unusual accessories, art, tables & desks, and even a frog in a bikini who'll croak if no one comes along and buys him. They also have a wish list on their website where you can request, say, an elephant head cachepot. Oh, wait, they have that already!

SHOP NEARBY: Less than 5 minutes away at 1194 Old S. Dixie Highway is **GRAPES,** another furnishings and home décor emporium. You can get a feel for what's there by going to their website (www.grapesfurniture.com) and seeing what they carry, from dining room sets to lighting to art to rugs to weird but adorable handmade dolls and more. But it would be a lot less frustrating if they would simply remove the photos of what was sold instead of aggravating us by showing something great at a good price that you need and then constantly saying "SOLD." Grrr.

TRUE TREASURES CRYSTAL TREE PLAZA

www.truetreasuresinc.com; Facebook: True Treasures Antiques //
1201 US Hwy., Suite 15 / North Palm Beach 33408 / (561) 625-9569
/ OPEN: Mon-Sat. 10-6; Sun. 12-5.

The most upscale of the three True Treasures, this one is for the connoisseur who likes to browse where great art, Persian rugs, fine china, and unusual antiques mingle with contemporary furniture. While some of it may take a chunk out of your budget, everything is worth it, and you'll be able to choose from their collection in a warm and delightful environment.

How do I know that what you'll buy here will hold up and still look good after a decade? I purchased my living room coffee table here 12 years ago, and it's in as good a condition as when I bought it. (And I get lots of compliments on it.)

NOTE: TRUE TREASURES also has a shop at 3926 Northlake Blvd., in Palm Beach Gardens and a new one in Delray.

TWINKLE ROCK

Twinklerock.com; Facebook: Twinkle Rock Kids Consignment//
9269 Prosperity Farms Rd. / North Palm Beach 33410/ (561) 837-3294 / OPEN: Tues.-Fri. 10-5; Sat. 10-3

Parents (and parents-to-be): Go a quarter of a mile north of North Lake Boulevard and you'll find a children's consignment shop that has everything for every age and every "stage."

Their merchandise starts with maternity clothes, and then on to nursery necessities, followed by boys and girls clothes from childhood to tween. Plus you'll also find playthings and books—even dancewear—that will appeal to all ages.

BARGAIN SAVING TIP:

Consignment shops are good to go to any time of the week, but generally, you'll find more on sale toward the end and beginning of the month. Many put clothes out at the beginning of each month and need to get rid of older merchandise first.

Thrift shops usually have the best bargains early in the week when they put most of their merchandise out. They also often have specific sales starting on Mondays, like shoes at 50% off. By Wednesday, or even Tuesday, the good ones may be gone.

&)(2

"I want someone to look at me the way I look at a Chanel."

—Stephanie Carina

&)(3

Lake Worth & Lantana

℘℘℘
LAKE WORTH'S LAKE AVENUE: HOUSEHOLD DÉCOR, FURNITURE, GIFTS & WOMEN'S CONSIGNMENT SHOPS

A four-block stretch of Lake Avenue right off Dixie Highway is becoming *the* place for people looking to decorate their homes—and themselves. There are over a dozen consignment clothing, furniture, home décor shops, art, galleries, crafts, antique malls, and more here. There's also the Cultural Council of Palm Beach County in a beautiful Streamline Moderne building at 601 Lake Avenue, and they always have interesting exhibits, plus a shop that carries local fare.

AFFLUENT FINDS

www.affluentfinds.com // 810 Lake Ave. / Lake Worth 33460 / (561) 588–7772 / OPEN: Mon.-Sat. 11-6; Sun.12-5

Affluent Finds is truly a fantastic women's consignment filled with designer labels at affordable prices. The owner, April Willis, handpicks each of the items, and there is always new merchandise.

Once there it's priced at about 50% off retail, or more, and you can even do even better in the sale section. The clothes are all in pristine condition; well organized and easy to find on the racks, with one in the center displaying the sale items. There's also plenty of nice jewelry, sunglasses, and handbags.

The fun starts even before you enter. The fetching window display often contains the newest arrivals of high-end accessories and apparel, so start by looking at that. Once inside you may notice that

Affluent Finds appeals to a broader age base than many of these consignments. Indeed, they carry something for every group, from the fun and fashionable sporty teen to the classic more sophisticated lady. Like the owner.

HOME ACCENTS SHOP NEARBY: A few doors down at 804 Lake Avenue **is ELENA'S "CHERRY PICKINGS,"** antiques & interiors. This large home décor and small furniture emporium also has five cases of jewelry, specializing in silver/Mexican. www.cherrypickingsantiques.com, OPEN: Mon.-Sun 11-6

ALL GOOD THINGS

328 N. Dixie Hwy. / Lake Worth 33460 / (561) 547-7606 / OPEN: Tue.-Sat. 10:30-5:30; Sun. 12-5

This charming country-style antique mall is much larger than it looks at first. That's because the front rooms are just for starters. Keep going, and you'll find not only more rooms but an outdoor back annex, and a high-end antique shop/watch repair in a separate shop to the left. Most of this mall is indoors, but the front rooms are surprisingly sunny for an antique mall. That gives it a warm feeling when you wonder through the 8,000 square feet of hidden treasures in this 19-year-old emporium. The brightness is one reason for the cheerful vibes at All Good Things, as is the friendliness of the owner, Doralea Asher, and the people who work there.

There's great diversity with 20 different dealers and something wonderful pops up at every turn. Many of the prices posted by the couple of dozen exhibitors are enticingly low to encourage turnover. "We turn and burn," says the entrepreneurial Doralea.

All Good Things is about half-and-half antique and collectibles, with plenty of smart inexpensive vintage jewelry. There's also a cottage out back in the patio area that is filled with even more antiques and collectibles You'll also find an entire section of shabby-chic furniture – which they'll repaint for customers at a low price. *NOTE*: Slightly south and to the back of All Good Things is DEVINE, a fresh produce market which also has a juice and smoothie bar.

BKG GALLERIES

www.brucekodner.com // 32 S. Dixie Hwy. / Lake Worth 33460 / (561) 533-7707 / OPEN: Mon.-Wed. 10-5; Thurs.10-8; Fri. & Sat. 10-5; Sun. 11-5

This is another place that can be hard to find—but once you do, it's well worth it. You'll find it slightly south of Lake Avenue, but even after you enter the parking lot, you might accidentally go straight ahead to the auction galleries. NO. Turn left at the red door and you'll be rewarded with a trip through four large rooms overflowing with fabulous antiques, collectibles, costume and real jewelry, a bit of vintage clothing and just about everything else.

I always find something when I'm there, wandering through their elegant furnishings. Their specialties include furniture, jewelry, vintage clothing, crystal, silver, pottery, linens, artwork, toys, decorative accessories, antiques, and much more!

There are more than 70 diverse dealers so there is plenty to choose from. Some of the "real stuff" is behind glass, but they'll quickly and cheerfully come and open it up for you. Many of the items in the open and closed booths also have sale signs, which is a joy to see.

BULLDOGGERS

www.bulldoggersantiques.net // Facebook: Bulldoggers Antiques // 201 Federal Hwy. / Lake Worth / (561) 312-6732 / OPEN: Mon.-Fri. 10-5; Sat. Sun. 12-5

A wonderful addition to Lake Worth is a couple of blocks off Lake Avenue but well worth the trip. Bulldoggers Vintage & Antique is much larger inside than it looks and carries everything from collectibles for a few dollars to a bronze elephant for $3800.

These estate liquidators are located on the corner of 2nd Avenue & Federal and parking is in the back. They also buy anything from one item to entire estates.

CARIELLE'S CLOSET

Carriellescloset.com, Facebook: CarriElle's Closet//9 N. K St. / Lake Worth 33460 /(561) 288-6694 / OPEN: Mon.-Sat. 12-7; Sun. 12-3:30

This is the latest entry in a town that already has a few great clothing resale shops, not to mention the art shops, craft stores, antique mall and the wonderful Cultural Council building.

The colorful clothes in this small shop pop out at you immediately as you walk in and survey the scene, taking in the attractive women's clothing, handbags and jewelry. There is a bit of retail, but most is resale which they buy outright. Their appeal is to a wide audience age-wise (35-85) style-wise (classic to current) and size-wise (petite to plus sizes). "Our clientele is anybody who appreciates quality, and like us, has a passion for fashion," say the two women, whose names are Carrie and Elle (get it?).

These two friendly owners are experienced retailers/resalers, having driven a truck (!) all over Southeast Florida selling their eye-catching apparel. They will be expanding and soon they'll be able to offer even more. For now, they've settled here as the newest clothing consignment entry in the county. You can find them on a side street off Lake Avenue right near two popular restaurants, Brogue's and Dave's Raw Bar.

NEW SHOP NEARBY: A new Estate Liquidator just opened up around the corner at 716 Lake Avenue: CAROUSEL GALLERY.

CAROUSEL ANTIQUE CENTER

815 Lake Ave. / Lake Worth 33460 / (561) 533-0678 / OPEN: Mon.-Fri. 10-5; Sat. 10-5:30; Sun. 1-5:30

AS THIS BOOK WENT TO PRESS, CAROUSEL ANTIQUE CENTER ANNOUNCED THEY WERE CLOSING.

This is a two-story 12,000-square-foot antique mall with many exhibitors and a wide variety of merchandise, from the very old to the ...well, not that new. It is an antique mall, after all, although there are plenty of collectibles around for those who like their "antiques" newer.

The jewelry and silver showcases in the front area are always a treat to look at which I've been doing it for years, although not for the 28 years that they've been around. They have about 75% vintage decorative and collectibles and 25% antiques. Many of the prices are excellent – particularly for the 5 shelves in the upstairs section. That floor has a more open feeling than some antique malls since you can walk around and see—and touch—a lot of what's there.

The owner, Fred, works hard to keep his customers happy so make him (and yourself) happy by coming here.

CONSIGNMENTS BY SALLY

www.consignmentsbysally.com; Facebook: Consignments by Sally // Lantana Center, 306 W. Mango St. / Lantana 33462 / (561) 547-4848 / OPEN: Mon.-Sat. 10-5:30

Even if you're not in the market for stunning furniture, art deco, glassware, unique household accessories or charming and unusual gifts, you must come to Sally's to look at her collection. Sally has been in the business for 20 years, and she knows what she's doing. Everything in her shop looks new and take-home wonderful. She has décor for every taste, and you might end up with something smashing for that lonely corner in your home that's begging to be filled.

Everyone likes doing business with Sally and her daughter Barbara. I often come there just to say hi and see what's new (lots, generally) at

the 3,400-square-foot three-part store. They probably have more giftware, household accessories, and accent pieces—many quite amusing– than other similar furniture consignments, maybe more than most new gift shops as well. They also pick up and deliver.

HOW TO GET THERE: You may pass this mall without realizing it's there. Going south on Dixie, make a right on Ocean Avenue in Lantana, cross the railroad tracks, and then make an immediate left. Sally's is at the far end.

FASHION EXCHANGE

702 Lake Ave./ Lake Worth 33460/(561) 547-9521/OPEN: Mon.
Tues. Thurs. & Sat.10-5; Wed. & Fri. 10-7; Sun. 12-5.

This is another place I've been happily coming to for decades. So I know why this women's and men's consignment shop is sometimes called "The Jewel of Lake Worth."

Owned by Judy King since 1989, it's well-stocked with designer-label clothes for men and women along with women's accessories. The prices are usually far lower than what you'll spend for similarly consigned clothes and accessories in nearby Palm Beach. How much lower? A Judith Leiber bag selling for $1,000 on the island was $400 here. Not bad!

Fashion Exchange also has more hats than most resales—it's worth coming there just to see those fashionable chapeaus—plus a few sections of good men's clothes, something you don't find in many places. They also have nice furs, and a large jewelry selection in a revolving display.

DON'T MISS: All the way in the back, behind the shoe section, you may find some more goodies.

PLATO'S CLOSET

www.platosclosetboyntonbeach.com; Facebook: Platos Closet
Boynton Beach FL // 701 N. Congress Ave., Bay 3B / Boynton
Beach 33426 / (561) 369-3550 / OPEN: Mon.-Fri. 10-8; Sat. 10-6;
Sun. 12-5

The emphasis here is on the mostly overlooked resale buying group: teens. All Plato's are stuffed with teen-oriented selections, and going through the racks, you'll spot many "younger" high-cred brands, like Aeropostale, Baby Phat, Bebe, Diesel, Ecko, Gap, Limited, Old Navy, Rampage, and the ubiquitous Forever 21. They claim to sell "fashion-savvy clothing for teens and young adults (men and women), promising "gently-used brand-name clothing and accessories"—shoes, purses, belts, jewelry, jeans—that have been purchased within the last year.

Sizes for men and women are generally smaller than most resales, and you'll also find lots of jeans and heels so high you can dizzy looking at them, nonetheless wearing them.

Most of it is quite inexpensive. That's why the teen-centric resale concept works so well that they have hundreds of franchises throughout the country.

NOTE: They buy everything outright with immediate payment. But some sellers have complained that you get so little for an item, they're almost better off donating them to a thrift shop and taking a deduction. SALE INFORMATION: They have seasonal clearances announced at their website. Sign up.

NOTE: Here are some additional Plato's Closets in Palm Beach County. Call before going because these are franchises so stores change more than regular ones. BOCA RATON 2240 NW 19th St. / (561) 392-7075 // PALM BEACH GARDENS 11686 US Hwy. 1 / (561) 625-0059 // WELLINGTON 10200 Forest Hill Blvd., Suite 110 / (561) 422-3838.

SEQUELS BOUTIQUE (Now ZASU BOUTIQUE)
617 Lake Ave. / Lake Worth 33460 / (561) 586-0004 / OPEN: Mon.-Fri. 11:30-5:30; Thurs.-Sat. 11:30-6:30; Sun. 1-4

Sequels is a combination of consignment (on the right side) and new, (on the left). It's a large shop and you might find something in either area. I spotted a stunning turquoise brand new Badgley Mischka bathing suit priced at an unbelievable $18, but, of course, it was not my size. They carry a lot of mid-range brands (Juicy Couture, Chico's,) and shoes at good prices, plus a selection of unexciting accessories such as handbags, jewelry, belt, and scarves.

SHOP NEARBY: Next door at 615 Lake Avenue is **LAKE WORTH JEWELERS,** which sells much more than just jewelry. Ella Riggs, whom everyone in the neighborhood knows and likes, has stocked this shop with stunning Mary Frances handbags, outrageous hats, and truly outstanding costume and fine jewelry. If bling is your thing, this is the place to come.

SHADES OF TIME

www.shadesoftimeonline.com; Facebook: Shades Of Time// 214 E. Ocean Ave. / Lantana 33462 / (561) 540-8925 / OPEN: Tues.-Sat. 9:30-5; Sun. Mon. 9:30-2:30

They've been in business for over 20 years, and they're the last remaining independent sunglass shop in the county. They sell thousands of them in this small shop, including those of major designers, all discounted with prices ranging from $39-$500.

HOME DéCOR SHOPS NEARBY: **CONSIGNMENTS BY SALLY'S** at Lantana Center, 306 W. Mango.

SILHOUETTES

Facebook: Silhouettes Consignment and Boutique "by Patti"/916 S. Dixie Hwy./ Lantana 3346 / (561) 585-4343 / OPEN: Mon.-Sat. 10-5

I have been coming for years and have especially enjoyed it since the new owner, Patti, took it over. That's because shopping there is so simple. This is what a woman's consignment clothing shop should be like: a great selection at excellent (meaning low) prices, a store that's easy to walk around in yet is still full of lovely merchandise.

The clothes are divided not only by type but by color so it's easy to find what you're looking for. Want a green blouse? Find the green section fast and choose from many beautiful blouses. There's also a separate section for higher-end clothes by name designers. A section for Chico's. Lots of handbags and jewelry up front. And color coding that's easy to spot.

Happiness is when it's in your size—and on sale!

VITA NOVA

www.vitanovainc.org/ 3129 S. Congress Ave./Palm Springs 33461/ (561) 434-2754/ OPEN: Tues.-Sat. 9:30-6

This attractive stand-alone thrift in Palm Springs (north of Lake Worth) through good donations and excellent management has for years been one of the better quality resale shops.

It's in its own building and is just a medium-sized store, which carries a small amount of new clothes. Most of it is gently worn, although the "new" is priced almost as low as the "resale." The apparel is not what you should come here for. It's the smart, new-looking furniture, artwork, and home decor up front. *NOTE:* Some employees speak Spanish.

THE PAINTED OX

www.thepaintedox.com; Facebook: The Painted Ox // 5800 S. Dixie Hwy. / Lake Worth / (561) 598-8888 / OPEN: Mon.-Sat. 10-5:30; Sun. 12-5.

The Painted Ox is a different kind of furniture store emerging to take advantage of new painting techniques, modern fabrics, and the desire to put a little joy into decorating one's home. Lili Batista, store owner, and chief designer decided to take some of the best quality vintage pieces and update them to fit in today's coastal homes.

Now, Lili finds vintage pieces and re-imagines these pieces of art so that they will infuse character into a Florida residence. She strips them down, adds color and vibrancy, and prices them to sell. "People often say the prices are too low, and maybe they are," she said. "But the joy comes from sending off a finished chair, desk, table, or what-have-you to re-emerge into a new home, living life all over again. You could say the Painted Ox is the mechanism by which furniture is reincarnated," she added.

In this bright and beautiful two-part four-year-old 6,000-square-feet shop they'll gladly do "custom work for your tired old pieces" working with their fabric, upholstery and painting on site. The new piece, as they like to say there, is "thinking outside the ox."

WORLD THRIFT

www.redwhiteandbluethriftstore.com/Lake_Worth.html // 2425 N.
Dixie Hwy. / Lake Worth 33460 / (561) 588-4050 / OPEN: Mon.-Sat.
9-6. *Note: cash only*.

World Thrift is the shrine where all area thrifties (often secretly) come to worship. Many swear by (some at) this huge warehouse for orphaned clothes, some of which are practically given away at mind-boggling hard-to-believe prices. But it's not for the faint-hearted; only intrepid shoppers dare to enter.

Here's the good part. World Thrift is a clean, well-lit thrift shop with clothes neatly on the hangers. Cashiers move the lines quickly, except for Wednesdays, which is senior sale day, and Saturday morning after 10. There's a tremendous turnover in merchandise, so even those who go a few times a week—and there are plenty of regulars—constantly find new bargains.

OK, now for the bad reports. It's so large, and clothes are divided according to type (say, blouses, short sleeves), and then color, but it's all mixed in. That means shoppers have to spend inordinate amounts of time going through everything if they're looking for a specific item in a certain color. This makes shopping hard work instead of play, although some love this kind of activity.

Some of the clothes have mild damage, or are missing buttons, or no size is listed, or something is slightly wrong with it, so everything must be examined carefully. Smelled, also. Although they usually don't have that budget thrift shop turn-off smell when you enter, some of the clothes do have a faint odor, especially after they've been in stock for a few days.

One more thing: the better handbags up front are sometimes fake, so you have to examine them carefully. (See Boca Raton chapter on nine ways to tell if a handbag is real.)

NOTE: There are no dressing rooms, so wear a bathing suit or camisole underneath your clothes so you can try things on publicly.

SALE INFORMATION: There's a big sign in back of the row of cashiers telling you what color is either on sale or excluded from the sale that day. Wednesday is 50% off for seniors 55+ except for the color of the day.

SHOPS NEARBY: ONE MORE TIME! THRIFT SHOP AND COFFEE BAR. See Part IV on Thrift Shops. Also, if you're looking for jeans and can't find one here – almost impossible with their huge selection – go north on Dixie to the GOODWILL at 3622 South Dixie Highway. They have a large selection of mid-level jeans. "The very expensive ones go to the boutique shops, but we get them in the low and medium range," said one of the managers.

DONATE YOUR CLOTHES TO HELP A WOMAN GET A JOB...PLUS "TIEBERRIES" HELP A MAN FOR HIS JOB INTERVIEW:

"Dress for Success" works with others to give women the proper clothes to wear for a job interview. Then, if she gets the job, they give her enough clothes for her first week at work! The local affiliate of this nationwide nonprofit organization is at 118 East Ocean Avenue in Lantana. Call (561) 249-3898 for an appointment to donate.

What does a man do who has a job interview and doesn't have a tie? Why he goes to a library of course. Not to read a book—alas, few people do that anymore. No, to borrow a tie for up to three weeks. Unfortunately, he has to go to Queens, New York to do this since Tieberries are only in four Queens libraries right now. Hopefully, the idea will spread to Florida soon.

Palm Beach

SPECIAL PALM BEACH SHOPPING TOUR—

ONE BLOCK OF UPSCALE CONSIGNMENT SHOPS

The eastern end of Sunset Avenue/North County Road in Palm Beach with seven shops all clustered together is the Holy Grail for consignment shoppers. The stores start at the end of North County Road, and then circle around to Sunset Avenue. Recently, another great shop, Annexe de Luxe arrived at Sunrise Avenue, a block away, so start your tour from there. (A description of all these shops are in this chapter.)

ANNEXE de LUXE (Paradise Lost) at 227 Sunrise Avenue.

CLASSIC COLLECTIONS at 118 N. County Road.

RAZAMATAZ at 208 Sunset.

EMBASSY BOUTIQUE (GOODWILL) at 210 Sunset.

ATTITUDES at 212 Sunset.

MAXIM'S of **PALM BEACH** at 212 Sunset or 219 Royal Poinciana Way.

PARADISE LOST at 210 Sunset, (also 219 Royal Poinciana Way #3) across from MAXIM'S.

CASSIE & JAMES BOUTIQUE is in the via between MAXIM'S and PARADISE LOST at 219 Royal Poinciana Way #2 (also 2 Via Testa).

FOR A SECOND PALM BEACH SHOPPING TOUR, SEE PAGE 59.

ATTITUDES CONSIGNMENT BOUTIQUE

www.attitudesofpalmbeach.com; Facebook: Attitudes Of Palm Beach // 212 Sunset Ave. / Palm Beach 33480 / (561) 832-1666 / OPEN: Mon.-Sat. 10-5

Occasionally, you'll spot a lovely sight here: a brand new garment with the tag still dangling from it. Whether or not it's got that tag, for those looking to splurge, there are designer heavyweights like St. Johns and Chanels sprinkled in among their clothes and handbags. And they're about one-third the regular price.

You'll also find some footwear here, often even Stubbs & Wootton shoes, worn by the Palm Beach fashion cognoscenti. Among other unique items: sometimes you'll see equestrian pants for the horsey set, plus ski and winter jackets for the snowbirds.

NOTE: Parking on Sunset is for one hour only and is strictly enforced. If you get carried away and forget to move your car, what you bring home from your shopping expedition may be an expensive parking ticket.

BALATRO VINTAGE GALLERY

408 Hibiscus / Palm Beach 33480 / (561) 832-1817 / OPEN: Mon.-Sat. 10-6, or by appointment.

Behind Chanel is this high-end vintage clothing emporium that carries separates, gowns and even costumes that are only top of the line. "If I find something good enough I'll put it in here," says the owner, Tiffany who, with her mother, hand chooses everything that ends up in this very pricey shop. They specialize in super-expensive vintage Chanel & Dior—mostly French and a few English high-end designers, all in perfect condition. Also around the room, nestled in various boxes, cabinets, and displays is an impressive selection of vintage jewelry, such as Miriam Haskell and Chanel.

CASSIE AND JAMES BOUTIQUE

Facebook: Cassie and James Boutique // 219 Royal Poinciana Way, #2 (or 2 Via Testa) / Palm Beach 33480 / (561) 366-8466 / OPEN: Tues.-Sat. 10:30-5

This is a very small shop that packs a big punch. On a via off Sunset, right past **PARADISE LOST**, it's filled with many great things, some for children but mostly for adults. While it's the only consignment shop in the area that stocks any children's clothes and accessories, what's here would mostly appeal to their parents, and even those without children.

The friendly owner, Susan, uses Facebook to announce sales and new items that have come in. So join the Facebook Page for additional Sale and Discount information.

CHURCH MOUSE

www.bbts.org/about-us/church-mouse; www.facebook.com/ pbchurchmouse // 378 S. County Rd./Palm Beach 33480 / (561)659-2154 / OPEN: Mon.-Sat. 10-4

This shop is indisputably the best thrift shop in all of Palm Beach County—perhaps any place in the world—for high-end clothes at low-end prices. Not to mention all kinds of moderately-priced miscellany for the home and person.

This bustling eight-room shop is filled with what used to be in some of the finest Palm Beach homes (and closets) and is now being sold at

prices that are amazing for what you get. Particularly outstanding are the women's evening gowns immediately to the right when you enter. In the back to the right, they also have a large alcove for superb men's clothes, all like new and many with expensive labels.

Elsewhere you'll find good women's tops, jackets, slacks, shoes, and books, magazines, children's clothes, toys, DVDs, home and kitchen do-dads, pillows, small appliances, glassware, and whatever else they acquire from local donations. The proceeds go to Palm Beach's Bethesda-by-the-Sea Church, which became world-famous when Donald Trump married Melania there in a wedding whose guests included Arnold Schwarzenegger, Rudy Giuliani, Chris Christie, P. Diddy, Steve Wynn, Derek Jeter, Don King, Matt Lauer, Billy Joel, Kathie Lee Gifford, Simon Cowell, Paul Anka (who complained that he was seated behind a pillar during the ceremony) Kelly Ripa—and Bill & Hillary Clinton.

DON'T MISS: Don't miss the sale notice by the entrance listing the day's colored-ticket code.

NOTE: Church Mouse closes in June; opens in October. While you're waiting for it to reopen, note that the jewelry outlet shop SEQUIN is a block away at 330 S. County Road.

CLASSIC COLLECTIONS—PALM BEACH
www.classiccollectionsofpalmbeach.com;
Facebook: Classic Collections of Palm Beach // 118 N. County Rd./ Palm Beach 33480 / (561) 833-3633 / OPEN: Mon.-Sat. 10-5:30

This designer and high-fashion resale boutique has some new clothes mingled in with the rest. Whatever is there is very pricey—as one would expect with racks of St. Johns and Chanels. They're still way under the original cost.

Still, there are some less expensive items. Sure, they have Judith Leiber bags and Chanel quilted purses for $1,000+ each. But they've also carried a Kate Spade shoulder bag for $50 and a Pucci purse for $190.

There's usually a rack or two in the back section where you may find some markdowns. But it's still not a place for the budget conscious. Occasionally, there are a few furs, and there is always stunning jewelry under glass, originals as well as consigned. To the side are luxury shoes, like Chanel, Manolo Blahnik, Jimmy Choo, Gucci, Prada, Yves St. Laurent, and other big names in fancy footwear, all as attractive as is everything else in this shop.

EMBASSY BOUTIQUE GULFSTREAM GOODWILL
www.gulfstreamgoodwill.com/index.cfm // 210 Sunset Avenue / Palm Beach 33480 / (561) 832-8199/OPEN: Mon.-Sat. 9-5; Sun. 10-5

Goodwill pulls out some of the highest quality donations they receive and places them in this three-room store. In fact, you occasionally see some of the same garments here as in the nearby upscale consignments. That's because some of the owners of those shops donate their unsold merchandise to Goodwill if they didn't move in their own places.

Naturally, the clothes are not as deftly displayed, and they're usually not in as pristine condition as at the other nearby resales. But even superb condition Brooks Brothers tuxes have been just one of the finds among the very large selection of men's clothes here. And you'll always find plenty of women's clothes at Embassy Boutique, ranging from casual to couture, from low to standard price.

The better women's clothes and accessories are to the right in the front room in three open "closets." Shoes are straight ahead, and jewelry is under glass in various showcases. Higher-end accessories and handbags may be hanging in back of the register but look at the purses closely to make sure they're real.

DON'T MISS: The windows up front are very small and you can only see the merchandise from the outside. Some of it is very good, so stop and look before you enter. Also, don't breeze through the second section because there's a lot stuffed in here. Some shoes, for example, are almost hidden above and below the clothes.

SALE INFORMATION: The price tags attached to all garments have a colored string which is the color reduced that day. The sign explaining the color code is usually in front of the register. Plus, Wednesday is always Senior Day with 25% off everything.
SHOPS NEARBY: Nothing as inexpensive.

FOUR TIPS FOR CONSIGNING YOUR CLOTHES

1) The better the shop and the better the neighborhood, the more money they'll charge for your clothes and the more you will get from a consignment.
2 Call and find out when a shop is accepting consignments. Just because they're open doesn't mean they're doing consignments that day. You don't want to have to drag everything back home.
3) Look at your contract carefully and see how long they will hold something and when you have to pick up what they didn't sell.
4) Dress well and bring everything to consign in nice bags, boxes or suitcases. (Louis Vuitton luggage is always nice.) People have been known to bring clothes in to consign in garbage bags, giving the shopkeeper the immediate impression that they're trying to get rid of garbage!

SECOND PALM BEACH SHOPPING TOUR

There's a second lesser-known Mecca for resale and outlet lovers near Worth Avenue and a few minutes away from the Sunrise/Sunrise Consignment shops reviewed in this chapter.

Start at: **CHURCH MOUSE**, a high-end (quality) thrift shop at 378 S. County Road. Then go slightly north to **SEQUIN of PALM BEACH**, a jewelry outlet at 330 S. County Road. And finally, there's **FASHIONISTA**, a very pricey women's consignment shop at 298 S. County Road. (Stop at Classic Bookstore at 310 South County Road between Sequin & Fashionista.)

FOR ANOTHER SHOPPING TOUR OF PALM BEACH
CONSIGNMENTS, SEE PAGE 54.

FASHIONISTA

Facebook: Fashionista Palm Beach // 298 S. County Rd. / Palm Beach 33480 / (561) 249-6302 / OPEN: Tues.-Sat. 10–6

This shop is so exclusive that there's no way to know from the door or window that it's resale. They're so discreet they're not even with the other consignments on Sunset/North County Road. But those who sneak off to this posh consignment and vintage shop will pay for the privilege of getting the best and the most expensive. This is definitely one of the most upscale (expensive) consignment shops in three counties, with plenty of merchandise to choose from. If luxury is your game, and money not a consideration, this is your place.

MAXIM'S OF PALM BEACH

212 Sunset, or 219 Royal Poinciana Way, Via Testa #5 / Palm Beach 33480 / (561) 683-8181 / OPEN: Mon.-Sat. 10-5

As soon as you enter Maxim's designer boutique, with the chandeliers reflecting off mirrored walls illuminating the French lilac interiors, you feel the elegance and glamor of old Palm Beach.

This is one of the finest consignment clothing shops, and it's moved to a new location along with the other ritzy resales on Sunset.

Managed by the owner and a staff who have over 50 years combined experience in haute fashion, they're poised to assist you in choosing just the right look for any occasion—from classic casual to daytime chic to the most elegant evening ensemble.

Accessories anyone? Whether it's an ultra-smart Chanel handbag for your next luncheon, with a pair of Louboutin pumps, and bejeweled Judith Leiber earrings for your next charity event, you'll find these and the most desirable names in shoes, bags, scarves, belts, hats and jewelry right here.

SHOP NEARBY: **PARADISE LOST,** with unique home accents and clothing, is directly across the way on the via. (See "**Two Outstanding Palm Beach Shops.**")

RAZAMATAZ CONSIGNMENT BOUTIQUE

208 Sunset Ave. / Palm Beach 33480 / (561) 655-2135 / OPEN: Mon.-Sat. 10-5

This consignment boutique no longer has any relationship to the Boca Razzamataz, which has a different spelling anyway to make sure you don't confuse them.

This one, a 20-year-old small but beautiful shop, is also easy on the eyes—not so much the wallet. As you walk around, you'll encounter upscale designer blouses, slacks, skirts, evening gowns, sunglasses, handbags and jewelry here (at upscale prices).

They sometimes carry furs, and while they'll warm you up, they may put a chill in your bank account.

They have a back room that they don't advertise or even tell their customers about, and if you're lucky, it will be open. If it is, you'll find some excellent bargains on garments that didn't sell up front.

SEQUIN PALM BEACH

www.sequin-nyc.com; Facebook: Sequin Palm Beach // 330 S.
County Rd. / Palm Beach 33480 / (561) 833-7300 / OPEN Mon.-Sat.
10-6; Sun.11-6.

For twenty years they only sold their popular costume jewelry
bracelets, earrings, necklaces and more to some of the larger
department stores such as Henri Bendel, Saks, and Nordstrom. But
now they sell some of the same pieces direct to customers—at a
much lower price.

The cheery and colorful two rooms display everything well, and
you'll want to buy all of it: starting with the cheaper bangles in the
first room to the pricier jewelry such as the "statement necklaces" in
the back.

"We're like a rock concert in here," one of the saleswomen said to
me, trying to convey the excitement and the amount of people
crowded around the jewelry. True. Just look at the excited faces of
the shoppers! Or forget the shoppers and just look at the jewelry!
Owner Kimberly Renk is well-liked and well-known in town,
especially for her charity work with pets. Her special love is for
rabbits, so don't be surprised if you see one there. And make like
them and hop on down here!

NOTE: There's a second **SEQUIN OF PALM BEACH** on Worth
Ave at # 219. They tend to have higher prices and bigger names, like
Badgley Mischka who has a line of Jewelry. Sequin also has a third
great shop in Delray, at the corner of Atlantic and Federal at 445 East
Atlantic Avenue.

ജ

*The quickest way to know a woman is to go
shopping with her.*

—Marcelene Cox

ജ

ℰᎧᏨ

HOW MANY SHOES DO YOU OWN?

The average woman owns 19 pairs of shoes and she bought her first pair without her mother at the age of 14. Even now she's pretty independent—or sneaky—about her shoe purchases, because one-quarter of the women admitted that they didn't tell their partners when they purchased another pair.

The survey, conducted by gocompare.com said that women will end up buying 469 pairs of shoes in their lifetime, and spending close to $25,000 on them. (Presumably, those buying at consignment or thrift will spend less!) So if you've bought close to 469 already, well, you were just setting yourself up for the rest of your life. But don't tell your partner about it.

ℰᎧᏨ

Gilding the Lilly (Pulitzer)

No designer is more quintessentially Palm Beach than Lilly Pulitzer. She started her career by running a fruit and juice stand. The bright pink, green, and pastel Lilly-look came about because she wanted colors and patterns strong enough to hide the stains when the food fell on her! Current Lillys can be found in many local venues, and a few places in this book also sell her vintage line.

ജ⏉ര

FOUR SPECIAL SALES IN PALM BEACH THAT YOU DON'T WANT TO MISS

1) **CHURCH MOUSE CLOSING SALE**: Early in June, the best thrift shop in all of Palm Beach County, the Church Mouse at 378 S. County Road, closes for the summer. The week before, everything goes on sale and is progressively reduced all week. (See Church Mouse listing in this chapter.)

2) **ST. EDWARD'S CHURCH:** This indoor/outdoor sale is held around Easter at the St. Edward's Catholic Church at 144 N. County Road.

3) **STUBBS & WOOTTON**: 4 Via Parigi: The Palm Beach "foot look" is either Gucci loafers without socks or Stubbs & Wootton slipper-like shoes with a distinctive logo. Stubbs & Wooten shoes regularly cost close to $400 each. But on the Monday after Easter, for one week, they're 50% off.

4) **C.ORRICO** at 336 S. County Road has had an annual Memorial Day Weekend sale for over 20 years. But they always have a great sale going on in their back rooms.

SPECIAL: If you want to buy something that says "Palm Beach" or "33480," the iconic zip code, go online to *www.palmbeachpurses.com* for totes with the town name, or *www.crescenttie.com* for a line of "33480" products.

ജ ര

PARADISE LOST

www.ParadiseLostPalmBeach.com; 214 Sunset Ave., or 219 Royal
Poinciana Way, Via Testa #3 / Palm Beach 33480 / (561) 223-2284 /
OPEN in Season: Mon-Sat 9:30-7; Sun. 12-6. Off Season: Mon.-Sat.
10:30-6; Sun. 12:30-5

Paradise Lost, the aptly named anchor shop on Via Testa, is a must-
see when visiting Palm Beach's famous Sunset Avenue consignment
district. The shop—well known to the international set (from Tanya
Pierce days) for fascinating gifts, objets d' art and home décor has
expanded into the only true emporium on Palm Beach Island.

In addition to Herend, Lalique and Waterford; English, French and
German china; and antiques, oils and sculptures, there are now full
men's and women's departments featuring designer shoes, clothing
and accessories, including bags, fine and costume jewelry and
luggage, much of it from homes on the island.

There is no other consignment shop in Palm Beach where one can
find, for instance, that definitive Cartier bracelet or Chanel handbag
for her, as well as that au courant Hermes necktie or pair of
Ferragamo loafers for him—and at the same time, purchase a couple
of polo mallets, a 17th century French painting, or a mounted John
Sutton Kerr safari head. The variety is incredible.

What you'll find here ranges from whimsical to wonderful—a
delightful blend of estate sale, fashion boutique, and museum. Leave
time enough to shop among familiar names: Louboutin, Prada,
Dresden, Gucci, Coach, Royal Copenhagen, Belleek, Versace, Royal
Crown Derby, Judith Leiber, Miriam Haskell, Zegna, Vuitton, Brioni,
Tod's, etc. And the endearing staff at Paradise Lost caters to every
need—all of us especially like Sean –helping each visitor to leave
completely satisfied and utterly delighted at the experience.

ANNEXE de LUXE (PARADISE LOST LUXURY ANNEX)

ANNEXE de LUXE www.paradiselostpalmbeach.com // 227 Sunrise Ave. / Palm Beach / (561) 223-2284 / OPEN: Mon.-Sat. 10-5; (Off Season: Thurs.-Sat. 10-5

This is the shop luxury-lovers have waited for. Here you will find more high-end accessories than anyplace in the county. Peek in the window and you can't wait to get inside. How gorgeous everything in there is! Plus the names! There's a Cartier section. A Tiffany one. Chanel—well, they never have fewer than 20 Chanel handbags. And kick up your heels because they have more Chanel shoes than they have at Chanel, not to mention the Louboutins, Choos and others.

It's not just their dazzling jewelry, handbags and shoes that fill the front that will get you. If you can tear yourself away, drift back, and you'll find racks of gorgeous almost-new designer clothes and furs. You'll recognize the designers: Hermes, Chanel, Pucci, Akris, Fendi, Cartier, Valentino, Oscar, Louis Vuitton, Gucci, Armani, Cavalli, Dolce & Gabbana, YSL, Christian Dior and many more.

Everything is well worth its price. Indeed, Owner, Sean, has been in the business a long time and accepts only authentic merchandise for consignment. He guarantees that everything sold here is absolutely real. (And might I add, *really beautiful.*)

FOUR MORE PALM BEACH PLACES WORTH VISITING

1. **GREEN'S PHARMACY OF PALM BEACH** is at 151 N. County Road, just a few blocks from the Sunset/Sunrise consignment shops, is an old-fashioned pharmacy with modern drugstore supplies, gifts and newspapers. But it also has a history. The coffee-shop style restaurant was where John F. Kennedy regularly had breakfast.

2. **CLASSIC BOOKSHOP OF PALM BEACH** is at 310 S. County Rd. In addition to a great selection of fiction and non-fiction books, in the center aisle are a large number of out-of-print books at greatly reduced prices.

3. **The PALM BEACH BOOKSTORE** is at 215 Royal Poinciana Way. Besides a great selection of fiction and non-fiction books, they have the largest section in Florida of books on interior design and architecture.

4. **SPRINKLES** Ice Cream & Sandwich Shop at 279 Royal Poinciana Way is under new ownership, but they still have the same great ice cream. Indeed, it was rated #1 in the country by *People* magazine, so try it!

NOTE: You can easily find parking on Royal Poinciana Way. If you park on the far side of the street, across from the grass divider, you get two hours instead of the one they give you directly across from the local restaurants.

Palm Beach Gardens

DÉJÀ VU ESTATE LIQUIDATORS

www.dejavuestateliquidators.com // 4086 PGA Blvd. / Palm Beach Gardens 33410 / (561) 225-1950 / OPEN: Mon.-Sat. 10-6; Sun. 12-4

If you're in the market for furnishings and/or home décor you *must* come to this mall, which not only carries the two incredible Déjà Vu Estate Liquidator shops, but two excellent smaller places where you can also find specialized merchandise to help you decorate your place and turn it into a showcase.

These four furnishing emporiums are in the same plaza where Loehman's once was, and if you don't remember where that was (how could we forget?) it's behind the Shell Gas Station on PGA & I-95.

DejaVu, which is relatively new, is really two galleries. On one side is the Annex, which looks like the main store although there are more sale and some smaller items here.

The main showroom—together the two take up 20,000 square feet—is mostly higher-end furnishings, although the prices are surprisingly low (and the level very high) for the excellent furniture, artwork, tableware and accessories that you'll find here.

There is also some jewelry in the glass cases, and off to the back is a lovely vintage alcove with handbags, shoes, and clothes, many with brand names like Gucci and Ungaro. They also have a large selection of furs there as well.

There's so much here that you may need help, and they have extremely friendly and knowledgeable people to assist you. For example, Inga, who assists customers with interior design as well as the vintage shop, was once the manager of Chanel in Palm Beach. Karl, the manager, is a trained art historian.

SHOP NEARBY: **THE FUNKY CRAB** at 4110 in this same old Loehman's mall is a bright and delightful new place with an enthusiastic and friendly owner. Patricia has filled two rooms plus two alcoves with fun vintage and coastal-inspired home décor plus repurposed furnishings, all waiting for enthusiastic buyers to take some of it home. And at those prices, they will.

All in all, there are lots of home and gift ideas, really reasonable prices, and reflecting the name of the shop, some unusual items here. (561) 662-4565. www.facebook.com/thefunkycrab

SHOP NEARBY: **INTERIORS SHOWROOM LLC**: For 25 years people looking for traditional furniture, especially couches and dining rooms sets with names like Baker, Drexel, Thomasville, Henredon, etc., have come here to 4118 in this same mall.   www.interiors-showroom.com / (561) 622-4100, Mon.-Sat. 10-5.

JENNIFER'S DESIGNER EXCHANGE

Facebook: Jennifer's Designer Exchange // 4401 Northlake Blvd. /
Palm Beach Gardens 33410 / (561) 459-7644
OPEN: Tues.- Sat. 10-5:30

Friends who like plush consignment shops keep asking me if I know about Jennifer's as if it's their own secret. How can you keep a place like this quiet?   The first time I went there—right after they had opened—all I could say was: "Where have you been all my life?" Well, my shopping life anyway. I would have been coming here for decades if only it had been around. That's especially true because there isn't a lot in the Palm Beach Gardens area for consignment clothing nuts, so this large luxury shop was a wonderful addition.

In fact, for those looking for higher-end consignment, it is definitely worth a trip just to come here. This large airy shop carries all the high-end designer clothes in perfect condition, and, yes, most of it is expensive–but exquisite. And probably never even worn.

Jennifer herself is not only friendly—not at all snobby—but knowledgeable, having once been the National Retail Director for designer apparel at Nordstrom. And now her shop ranks up there with the best. And priciest.

ഔരു

HOW JACKIE KENNEDY ONASSIS
MADE CONSIGNMENT SHOPS POPULAR

It wasn't always as acceptable as it is now to go to a consignment store. In the early '70's, there were only a few of them in the country, and going to a thrift store meant you couldn't afford to shop in a retail one.

But in the '70's, word got out that Jackie was secretly selling her new clothes at Encore, a consignment shop in Manhattan that was established in 1954. It seems that Jackie's super-rich husband, Aristotle Onassis, put her on a "strict" clothing allowance of $25,000 a month. She converted this to cash by buying expensive new clothes at Bloomingdale's, and then secretly having her secretary consign them at Encore.

Word leaked out, women went to Encore to buy Jackie's clothes, and suddenly it became fashionable to shop at consignments.

ഔരു

LADIES CHOICE

9339 Alt A1A, Suite #7B / Palm Beach Gardens 33403 / (561) 881-0302OPEN: Tues.-Sat. 10-5:30

You think of the word "jewel" the minute you walk in and look around – even before you learn that the owner's name is Jewel! She's owned this small but lovely shop for 21 years, during which time it has earned its excellent reputation by selling consistently attractive women's clothes at more than reasonable prices.

Another bonus is that it's very easy to navigate and you won't be tripping over clothes and struggling to find what you want. The rows of clothes can be easily found in racks down the middle and sides of the store. Accessories are in the middle, and in a showcase near the sales counter. All stores should be this well laid out!

MY FRIENDS CLOSET

4595 Northlake Blvd. / Palm Beach Gardens 33418 / (561) 622-3600
OPEN: Mon.-Fri 10-6; Sat. 10-4

This is a friend you want to have! This is a "closet" you want to visit. Once you walk in—it's in the back of this lovely mall—you'll see that everything is neatly organized not only according to size and type but also price. So you can hang out in the less expensive alcove, or visit the large upscale room to the right. Or you can ooh and aah over what's in the Accessories Room straight ahead. And in the showcase in the front area.

It's all neatly separated, making it easy to dive into what you want. For example, in the Accessories Room, there's a section of leopard skin, another of all green garments, and an area of new or almost new shoes.

They sell everything from Macy's to Valentino's, from small to size 2X, from affordable to high-end labels. This is a good "friend" to have.

RESTAURANT NEARBY: In this mall, already great with
RESALE THERAPY & JAMAR'S ENLIGHTMENT CENTER,
there's a wonderful and very popular seafood restaurant called
LOLA'S SEAFOOD EATERY.

RESALE THERAPY

www.resaletherapyshoppe.com; Facebook: Resale Therapy of Palm Beach Gardens // 4595 Northlake Blvd., Suite 113 / Palm Beach Gardens 33418 / (561) 691-4590 / OPEN: Mon.-Sat. 10-5

Starting with its clever name, right down to everything inside this shop, this place is outstanding. I fell in love with it the first time I found it and if I absolutely with difficulty had to find any fault with this place it's that it's so packed with marvelous things that getting around is a bit difficult.

Located two blocks west of I-95 at the Northlake Boulevard exit in Palm Beach Gardens, it's overflowing with high-end, new and vintage merchandise, from the useful to the unusual. That includes accessories, cabinets, tables, desks, lighting, glass, china, rugs, miscellaneous home décor, antiques, art and quality consignments, along with outright purchased items, all of which will turn your house into a home.

As for bargains, sign up for their mailing list and they'll let you know when they're having a sale. They also do room transformations, staging, design consultations, and professional organizing. (They cleverly call it "Outpatient Therapy.") And when you look at the job they've done to make this place beautiful, you can be confident that they'll do an outstanding job on your place as well.

SHOP NEARBY: If you're into New Age, a great shop is a few doors down: **JAMAR'S ENLIGHTENMENT CENTER** at Suite 107. They have a beautiful gift shop in the front room (the back is reserved for classes, with such top psychics as Michelle Whitedove). You'll find many wonderful and exotic gifts in this front room, along with handcrafted jewelry, paintings, statuary, healing stones, crystals and fascinating books like *The 100 Top Psychics & Astrologers in America.*

STYLE ENCORE
www.style-encorepalmbeachgardens.com; www.facebook.com/styleencorepalmbeachgardens //

4228 Northlake Blvd. / Palm Beach Gardens 33410 / (561) 223-2929/ OPEN: Mon.-Sat. 10-8; Sun. 11-6

This large spot in Gardens Towne Square can't easily be described as a "quality thrift" although it looks like that at first. But they stress that they're not a thrift (where people donate clothes) or a consignment shop (with better clothes since customers split the sale price) but a "resale" which buys clothes outright. Whatever.

What makes it strange, though, besides the clumsy name, is the juxtaposition of prices. Up front behind the large counter are some of the most expensive handbags you'll find in the county. There are at least two dozen such purses, casually strewn on top of each other, with price tags, like $4,500 for a Vintage Chanel and a Louis Vuitton vintage bag for $1500. This in a place where most of the items are under $25.

The clothes up front are also a bit more expensive, such as their over-priced Lilly Pulitzers. But get past the front section and there are rows of typical thrift clothes and shoes at reasonable prices.

Still, there are a few better items and designer labels mixed in, and you may see a colored tag on some indicating it's 40% off. I purchased a new Trina Turk top plus a sequined Clover Canyon blouse, each for under $40 and worth three times that.

There's another Style & Envy in Stuart, and both are owned by the same company that runs PLATO'S CLOSETS resales throughout the country. (See Lake Worth/Lantana chapter) The difference, they say, is that Plato's is for teens and these two are for adults.

NOTE: You can sell your clothes here and get money immediately, unlike a consignment shop where you have to wait to sell it...or a thrift shop where you get bubkis (that means "nothing").

SHOP NEARBY: Immediately next door is an unimpressive GOODWILL. You might be tempted to go in because of the sign outside saying that they have a vintage section. Don't waste your time. Except for a few dolls, most of what's in there fits the label of "ugly useless stuff from somebody's closet that no one wanted or needed any more that we're calling vintage."

TREASURES FOR HOPE

www.treasuresforhope.org // 3540 Northlake Blvd. / Palm Beach Gardens 33403 / (561) 691-8881 / OPEN: Mon.-Fri. 10-6; Sat. 10-4

This large stand-alone shop on Northlake came highly recommended to the Happy Shopper by a friend named Peggy who knows thrift shops. And when she said "this is one of the best thrift shops..." she knew what she was talking about.

Indeed, during a check there, a furniture buyer was eyeing the unique and incredibly inexpensive (for what you're getting) unusual items you could practically trip over, and she was positively swooning. "Whatever you say," she told me as she saw me writing notes, "you can't say enough good things."

With two exceptions: the clothes in a separate room were disappointing, very thrifty, and the few "boutique items" there barely warranted a second look. Nor did the two alcoves of children's toys, clothes, and miscellany for the tot set.

But the rest of it.... Furniture like a white $10,000 Roche Bobois couch in more-than-acceptable condition for $750. A group of Western home goods that included a rare real boot lamp. Who knows what you'll find in this large thrift shop but as Peggy promised, it's good enough to warrant a special trip there. The only sad thing is that most of us don't have room to take it home.

NOTE: My second and third check of this place were disappointing. There were far fewer items and higher prices. Did it become too popular?

TRUE TREASURES CONSIGNED FURNITURE & HOME DECOR

www.truetreasuresinc.com; Facebook: True Treasures Consigned Furniture & HomeDecor // Home Depot Center / 3926 NorthLake Blvd. / Palm Beach Gardens/(561) 694-2812 / OPEN: Mon.-Sat.10-8; Sun. 11-6.

If you asked a shopper in Palm Beach County the name of a place where you could buy great furniture and home décor, almost without hesitation most would say the name "True Treasures." True Treasures is definitely the best known in their area and so many  people have been very happy with their purchases there. (Count me as one.)

They have three emporiums now—that's how popular they are—and this one is conveniently located in the Home Depot Shopping Center. This immense 14,000-square-foot showroom is filled to the beautiful brim with attractive home furnishings.

The merchandise isn't grouped according to type, so you pretty much have to walk through the whole place if you're looking for something specific. But you won't mind because it's a true treasure to be in a community of practical, beautiful furniture and home décor that's in every style,very taste and is sure to be something you need and want.

ഇൗൽ

ESTATE SALES

If you're looking for estate sales, or you just like to traipse around lovely gardens in beautiful homes looking at nice things, then go to the *Palm Beach Daily News* classified ads for "estate" or "garage sales" listings, generally held before the upcoming weekend.

The owners who are trying to dispose of their fancy household goods, place many of the ads. But some people, like Lou Ann Wilson-Swan, put these sales together. Call her and she'll place you on her popular mailing list ("Lulu's Stuff") of upcoming estates sales. (561) 655-1529.

ഇൗൽ

74

WEST PALM BEACH & WELLINGTON

SPECIAL WEST PALM BEACH DIXIE HIGHWAY SHOPPING

Near Belvedere almost to Okeechobee on Dixie Highway are three shops located outside of Palm Beach, and the merchandise may be the same but the prices are often much lower.

Start at: **CITY GIRL CONSIGNMENT**, a women and children's consignment shop at 2900 S. Dixie Hwy....

NEARLY NEW is an upscale thrift shop at 2218 S. Dixie Hwy...

DINA C'S FAB & FUNKY BOUTIQUE at 1609 S. Dixie Hwy., Ste.#2, is a high-end women's vintage and consignment shop.

THESE SHOPS ARE DESCRIBED IN THE CHAPTER BELOW. FOR MORE STORES IN WEST PALM BEACH, SEE THE FOLLOWING LISTINGS.

ANTIQUE AND COLLECTIBLES SHOW AT THE SOUTH FLORIDA FAIRGROUNDS

www.wpbaf.com; Facebook: West Palm Beach Antiques Festival / 9067 Southern Blvd. / West Palm Beach 33411 / (561) 793-0333 / OPEN: On the first Friday, Saturday, and Sunday of every month.

For the last 18 years, the popular West Palm Beach Antique and Collectibles show has been held at the Americraft Expo Center, generally on Friday and Saturday from 9-5 and Sunday from 10-4:30. The monthly fairs are held in two large indoor rooms and a small outdoor section, where there are often some good buys, especially around the periphery. Don't miss the show in mid-February, when they have their annual giant Winter Spectacular and over 1,000 indoor and outdoor dealers come from all over the country. Thrifties might also want to keep their eyes open for the Fairground's occasional one-day garage sale.

NOTE: There are people who sell the same items at the fair as in their stores in Antique Row—but for less money. For example, D. Brett Benson sells his incredible vintage jewelry there as well as at his 3616 S. Dixie Highway shop (See Part III—Antique Row) & Gay Cinque sells the same trendy jewelry (a lot made by her) at the monthly shows as she does at her 1800 S. Dixie Highway store only she sells it for less at the fair.

HOW TO GET THERE: It's located off Southern Boulevard in West Palm Beach, 1.5 miles west of the Florida Turnpike and 1 mile east of 441/SR7.

ARISTOKIDS OUTPOST
Facebook: Aristokids Outpost // 6003 S. Dixie Hwy. / West Palm Beach 33405 / (561) 547-1737 / OPEN: Tues.-Sat. 10-5

How would you like to buy great children's clothes that were originally sold in the chi-chi town of Palm Beach at half the price? Then come to this small Dixie Highway outlet shop which offers 50% off brand new children and adult clothes from Aristokids, Girls Club, and Boys Club at 07/307a/309 South County Rd., in Palm Beach.

Newborn, children, and junior clothes are all represented in the racks. Squeezed next to those is a full rack of men's clothes to size 42, a revolving rack of miscellaneous sportswear for adult women, shoes, bathing suits, cover-ups and more—all at half price. Or more.

NEARBY SHOP: **NETTIE'S CONSIGNMENT** is somewhat junky-looking on the outside with its plastic chairs and low-end furniture, but inside are the contents of estates that they've purchased: mostly furniture, artwork, and jewelry, vintage and custom. Prices ranging from $1-$10,000 for merchandise within the 5,000-square-foot space which has a sort of garage sale/flea market look about it. Facebook: Netties Thrift Consignment /5404 S. Dixie Hwy. / West Palm Beach 33405 / (561) 202-7211 OPEN: Mon.-Sat. 11-6; closed Thurs., Sun.

BACK ON THE RACK

www.pbbackontherack.com; Facebook: Back on the Rack Consignment // 219 S. Olive Ave. / West Palm Beach 33401 / (561) 835-0006 / OPEN: Mon.-Sat. 10-6.

Nice consigned clothes and accessories with some new clothes mixed in at 25% off. Everything is reduced after 30 days and there's always racks of clothing at 50% off. Plus another rack of half off shoes. And even customer appreciation cards with discounts after you spend a certain amount there. And there's open on Sunday.

It sounds like consignment heaven. Except for one thing: location, location, location. It isn't in the heart of downtown (it's on the northwest corner of South Olive and Evernia Street), and parking is metered. If you do go, bring quarters.

SHOP NEARBY: **CLEMATIS STREET BOOKS & CAFE** at 206 Clematis Street is just a few blocks away and well worth the trip. It's a wonderful shop with quirky cards and great books, sweets, coffee and a real old-time General Store atmosphere you won't find elsewhere anymore. Come here to see it, as well as see what's in it.

CITY GIRL CONSIGNMENT

www.citygirlconsignment.com; City Girl Consignment//2900 S. Dixie Hwy./West Palm Beach 33401/(561) 820-0075/OPEN: Sun.-Fri. 10-5:30; Sat. 10-4

How do we love thee? Let us count the ways? First, City Girl has a beautiful assortment of women's consignment clothes and accessories. Then there are their prices, some of which are so low for what you're getting that it's hard to believe. ("Only $16 for that blouse? They've got to be kidding.") Add to  that a large shop with many rooms and a great assortment to choose from in many ranges, from the casual separates to upscale (but never outrageously expensive) gowns, to a large selection of belts and handbags that go from totally affordable and charming to Chanel behind a glass counter.

There are so many choices here—including a large selection of Lillys—all nicely displayed and separated according to type with room to wander around. It's almost impossible not to find something to fall in love with here. And that includes owner Tami, whom everybody loves. This place is, as the expression goes, to die. And, oh yes, the tags on the clothing are all color coded so the already low prices are often even lower.

THRIFT SHOP NEARBY: If you go north slightly past Belvedere on the east side of the Street is a pink awning. There's a great quality thrift shop there, **NEARLY NEW**.

CONNIE'S COLLECTION CONSIGNMENT BOUTIQUE

www.facebook.com/ConniesCollectionsConsignmentBoutique // 9859 Lake Worth Rd. / Wellington 33467 / (561) 964-0990 / OPEN: Mon.-Sat. 10-6

There aren't too many women's consignment shops in Wellington but this is almost worth a special trip. They have nice labels including plenty of Lilly Pulitzers and Chicos. Even furs in the winter. Also around were hard-to-find, one-of-a-kind unusual handbags by Mary Frances, Lulu Guinness, and Paloma Picasso, all in perfect-looking condition! All this plus plenty of bargains and clearance racks in the back.

That said, run, do not walk, to this place (OK, drive), as soon as possible.

CONSIGN AND DESIGN OF WELLINGTON

www.myconsiganddesign.com; Facebook: Consign And Design of Wellington // 13857 Wellington Trace / Wellington 33414 / (561) 798-5222 OPEN: Mon.-Fri. 10-6; Sat. 10-5

This place is expensive, but everything is negotiable and they have sporadic sales. There are a lot of lovely things to look at in the 4,000 square foot showroom which they claim is the largest high-end furniture consignment in the whole area. Another reason to go: if you're into horses, and knick-knacks and pillows with pictures of them on it, you'll enjoy all the equestrian accessories and décor.

NEARBY SHOP: **ELEGANT ESTATES** at 11260 Fortune Circle is another upscale home décor and furniture gallery where many items also have an equestrian theme. You can get an idea of what's there by going to facebook.com/elegantestateswellington / (561) 793-7332

DECOR ONCE MORE

www.decoroncemore.com; ww.facebook.com/decoroncemore // Fairfax Center 6758 N. Military Trail, /West Palm Beach 33407 / (561) 840-8858 / OPEN: Mon.- Sat. 10-7; Sun. 11-5

Lots of what you'd expect and a bit of what you wouldn't expect, like a Caribou Taxidermy Full Shoulder Mount ($1,195), perfect for people who'd rather bag a buck than a bargain.

This woman-owned estate-buying gallery carries a wide variety of high-quality lightly and slightly-used furniture, from vintage to modern with some occasional bargains, like coffee tables for $50.

You'll recognize names like Century, Drexel, Baker, Bernhardt, Lexington, and specialty items from designers such as Maitland Smith, Karl Springer, Milo Baughman, Vladimir Kagan, Ferguson Copeland and many other custom pieces.

DINA C'S FAB & FUNKY BOUTIQUE

www.fabandfunkyvintage.com; Facebook: Dina C's Fab & Funky Consignment Boutique; Twitter: @DinaCsFabFunky // 1609 S. Dixie Hwy., Suite #2 / West Palm Beach 33401 / (561) 659-1420 / OPEN: Mon.-Sat. 12-6

One of the best-liked women in Palm Beach opened up a high-end consignment shop that rapidly became one of the best-liked shops—especially because it's near the bridge for Palm Beach but the prices are better.

I have been coming here since Dina opened a few years ago, and have never seen an item there anyplace else! Dina herself dresses uniquely, in fab and funky, of course. She tells you that she's not looking for—nor does she wear—clothing and accessories that "are made in China."

Not only is Dina's place (and her clothes) unique, so is her family. When her daughter Lily was 10, she appeared on *David Letterman*'s show and also major magazines showing off her unusual talent of hypnotizing and dressing up the local lizards! They were then photographed, and developed into a cottage industry of greeting cards and T-shirts. (See Lizard-ville.com) And the little girl has grown up and is sometimes selling behind the counter!

NEARBY: **The Norton Museum of Art** at 1451 S. Olive Avenue.

KOFSKI ESTATE SALE

www.kofskiantiques.com; Facebook: Kofski's Antiques Inc. // 5501 Georgia Ave. / West Palm Beach 33405 / (561) 585-1976 / OPEN: From Dec.-May, approximately every 6 weeks.

Eager bargainers and determined dealers line up in the early morning hours, and by 10, a lot of the merchandise may have been sold. But the facility is huge—12,000 square feet consisting of two ample-sized rooms, an outdoor area, and "The Marketplace" across the street—so there will surely be some good décor left for you.

The atmosphere is very festive. When a piano is for sale, someone may be playing it, so it's more like a party than a sale. But then too, a sale is always a reason to party.

The inventory changes constantly, but includes large and small furniture pieces and home décor. Prices may start around $6 and go to thousands for antiques and decorative arts.

SALE INFORMATION: Many people don't realize that on Monday, if the merchandise didn't sell and is still available, it may be had for a better price, since Kofski is more open to negotiation at that time than at the height of the weekend.

HOW TO GET THERE: From Dixie Hwy., turn west on Bunker Rd. It's on the corner of Bunker and Georgia between Southern and Forest Hill.

NEARLY NEW

www.morselife.org/nearly-new-shop // 2218 S. Dixie Hwy./West Palm Beach 33401/ (561) 655-3230 /OPEN :Mon.-Fri. 9:30-5; Sat. 9-4; Sun. 12-4

If I could only go to one shop it might be this one. I've been coming here for years and I can practically never leave without buying something—and feeling I got a great buy to boot. They've got a little bit of everything, except high prices.

Most of what's in my shopping bag after I leave there are clothes or accessories. But when I moved to Florida (from NY) I bought a beautiful large framed Peter Max painting for $4,500—and it was appraised right afterward for $7,500—without a frame.

But it's the smaller items in this diverse treasure trove that should make this a big place on your list. (And it supports a good charity: MorseLife, which helps the needy in the community.)

Bottom line: Nearly New is a marvelous upscale thrift; clean and much bigger than it looks because of the large separate furniture room in the back.

My favorite is the alcove in the back to the right for boutique clothes, and I often find something for my husband in the men's department section up front to the right. I also like the fact that they always have sales going on and racks at practically give-away prices–making most things there a true bargain.

Plus, the manager here, Susan, is one of the best. NOTE: Parking is in the back.

"If men liked shopping, they'd call it research."

—P.J. O'Rourke

ON COURSE CONSIGNMENT SHOP

www.wellington-wef.com/on_course/business.html; Facebook: On Course Consignment Wellington // Wellington Plaza, 12773 W. Forest Hill Blvd., Suite 110 / Wellington 33414 / (561) 753-6256 / OPEN: Mon.-Fri. 10:30-5:30; Sat 10-6. Open Sun.

Could there be a successful consignment shop devoted to used equestrian tack and riding apparel for children as well as adults? Neigh-sayers (ha ha!) might say "no." But in Wellington, Florida, horse country, one can indeed find such a place. Just trot on down to "On Course," a small shop with interesting paraphernalia for the horse owner, rider, or just plain horse lover. They carry saddles, bridles, riding coats, jackets breeches, boots, children's riding apparel, blankets, ribbons, and cookies. For the horse, not the rider.

RED BALLOON &
RED BALLOON OF WELLINGTON

www.shopredballoon.com;
www.facebook.com/redballoonconsignment // 1800 Forest Hill Blvd. / West Palm Beach 33406 / (561) 966-7956 / OPEN: Mon.-Fri. 10-7; Sat. 10-5:30 & 9120 Forest Hill Blvd./ Wellington 33411 / (561) 333-2515 OPEN: Mon.-Fri. 10-6; Sat. 10-5:30

Their main store in a mall in West Palm Beach carries designer fashions and name brand labels for women and men, even though it got it started solely as a children's consignment shop. But the two large rooms now carry not only clothes but also an assortment of personal accessories, household décor and furniture.

Just eight miles west of their landmark store in West Palm Beach, Red Balloon has a second location in Wellington. Conveniently located near the Wellington Green Mall on Forest Hill Boulevard, they have attractively low prices for mid-level items. This one carries juniors instead of children's.

SHOP NEARBY: Wellington has a GOODWILL BOUTIQUE at 13873 Wellington Trace. They also have a PLATO'S CLOSET with teen-centric clothes at 10200 Forest Hill Boulevard #110.

THIS N THAT

www.thisnthatwpb.com; Facebook: This N That // 216 Clematis St. /West Palm Beach 33401 / (561)833-5223 / OPEN: Tues. Wed. Fr. 11-7; Thurs. 11-10; Sat. 10:30-6; Sun. 12-5

This place is a delightful surprise. First of all, who would have thought there would be a trendy affordable home décor—small furniture type place amidst all the entertainment venues on Clematis? (Actually, this place is also entertainment, since looking around is a wonderful way to spend time.)

The size of it is also a nice surprise, because there's only a small window on the street making you think it must be a really tiny place. But inside, it's long and narrow so the size of it and how much is in there is a pleasant surprise.

But the best surprise is all are the wonderful things inside– and at terrific prices. A lot of it tagged quite low, and even the more expensive items. are obviously worth much more. Besides furniture, there's everything from paintings to handbags making browsing there fun and as I said, entertaining. Not to mention rewarding, since you'll definitely find something interesting to buy. A special treat is to go here on a Saturday when you can also go to the nearby **Green Market** which runs from 8-2.

THREE THINGS YOU DIDN'T KNOW ABOUT BLUE JEANS

1) The average American owns seven pair of jeans.

2) Your jeans can make you sick. Too-tight jeans can lead to a nerve problem that causes numbness and burning. It's called the "tingling thigh syndrome."

3) If a man named Davis had $68 in 1883, jeans would be called "Davis's" instead of "Levi's." A dry-goods merchant named Jacob Davis invented "work pants" but didn't have the money to patent them. So he turned to rich businessman Levi Strauss, and they patented them together.

THE BEST WAYS TO SAVE
MONEY IN BROWARD

If you want to know where the bargains are—besides this book—start following (well, not literally) South Florida consumer expert Doreen Christensen. She hunts down the best dining and shopping bargains deals and steals on her Shop-O-Matic blog at Sun-Sentinel.com/Shop and in her Doreen's Deals column in the *Sun Sentinel* Money section.

Find more freebies and savings at Facebook.com/DoreensDeals and on Twitter @prettygoodideas.

A CONSIGNMENT GALLERY

www.aconsignmentgallery.com; facebook.com/aconsignmentgallery
Target Plaza, 3401 DC Country Club Boulevard., Suite #1 / Deerfield Beach 33442/(954) 421-2395 OPEN: Mon.-Sat. 10-6; Sun. 12-5

I have followed this shop through three addresses (the last was on Federal) and thought it could never get any better. But now in its

new location (in Target Plaza) it's the best—of just about any place. This is the most exciting (and colorful) home décor, accent and vintage clothing shop in two counties: Broward and Dade. (And the biggest too.)

Come here and you don't need to go anyplace else except for the wonderful A SUMMER PLACE (also in Deerfield) for your larger pieces. Go to both and you can decorate your home so it will look like it's straight out of

House Beautiful. And not only will your house be beautiful but you will be too, because A Consignment Gallery has a fabulous selection of jewelry, from totally affordable to behind-glass designer spectacular.

They also have two boutiques for designer clothes, and as you walk around (on beautiful for-sale carpets) you'll also see furs, dolls, clocks, bowls, glass and…well, just keep walking throughout this 18,000 square foot palace and you'll find everything you could ever want. It's almost all open so you are constantly coming upon something great. Says Billie, the manager for 22 years, "We have something for everyone, from traditional contemporary to modern to very high end. You'll find here what you won't see anyplace else!" That's for sure. Come here and share my excitement.

ANOTHER CHANCE

www.facebook.com/anotherchance.consignment // Victoria Plaza 6125 Stirling Rd. / Davie 33314 / (954) 584-5150 / OPEN: Tues.-Fri. 10-5; Sat. 10-4

Thanks to Karen, the owner, they have a really nice selection of women's and teens' consignment clothes. That includes some big-name designer handbags and shoes to the right past the checkout counter, where better accessories are offered at impressive (meaning good) prices.

There's a lot throughout and it's easy to keep discovering more. I once had to wait out a blinding rainstorm there and found things I had missed in the medium–sized area even after close to a half-hour there before. Karen always finds time to chat with her many customers— she has 4,000 active accounts. "Give people quality and good prices and they'll come back....and back." I always do—and so do many others.

Rule of life: if the shoe fits, it's ugly.

A SUMMER PLACE

www.asummerplaceconsignments.com; Facebook: A Summer Place Consignments // 131 E. Hillsboro Ct. / Deerfield Beach 33441/(954) 426-6106 / OPEN: Mon.-Sat. 10:30-5:30; Sun. 12-4

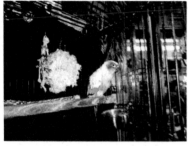

This is another place that's always on the top of my list of spots to go to again and again. It's a wonderful furniture and home décor spot in Deerfield Beach with an ample and interesting ten-thousand square feet of old and new gently-used accent pieces, lighting, rugs, jewelry, and handbags. Whether you need a living room set, dining or bedroom set, they have it all; plus tons of art, antiques, glassware and china.

It's a treat to walk through the many rooms because it's a gold mine of lovely furniture with good prices and friendly owners. (Look for Debbie).

A Summer Place is also in an interesting building. Indeed, it's one of the oldest in Deerfield Beach, and the rooms and nooks and crannies are great for placing all the wonderful pieces they bring in daily.

COUTURE UPSCALE CONSIGN

www.coutureupscaleconsign.com; Facebook: Couture Upscale Consign Instagram: CoutureUpscaleConsignftl/2939 N. Federal Hwy. /Fort Lauderdale (Oakland Park) 33306 /(954) 565-4348 / OPEN: Mon.-Sat. 11-6

They look almost like sisters, but they're a mother and daughter who together have made this two-room designer and couture upscale boutique quite unique. In their own words, they carry today's hottest styles from top labels at a fraction of the retail price. That includes women's fashions, formal attire, casual wear, designer handbags, shoes, and accessories.

As soon as you enter, you'll see their serious couture and high designer labels,

86

such as Hermes, Chanel, Louis Vuitton, Gucci, Prada, Pucci, Roberto Cavalli, and more. But if it's less expensive that you're looking for, you'll find several reduced racks in the second room, which generally contains the less expensive clothes, shoes, and handbags.

SPECIAL SALES: They advertise their sales on Instagram and to those who subscribe to their mailing list, and/or become Facebook fans.

FESTIVAL (SAMPLE ROAD) FLEA MARKET

www.festival.com; Facebook: Festival Flea Market Mall// 2900 W. Sample Rd. / Pompano Beach 33069 / (954) 979-4555 / OPEN: Mon.–Fri. 9:30–5; Sat. Sun. 9:30-6

This is the best discount mall in the country—truly heaven for the bargain shopper who likes to flea. The only thing you won't find here are high prices, and the low prices are even better if you take advantage of their coupons. Look for them at their website, Facebook page, and in the *Sun-Sentinel*. You can redeem them outside the most popular booth, (at least for women) YONIQUE COSMETICS. They have a huge inventory of brand makeup, hair products, and expensive skin lotions, although unfortunately they usually have huge check outlines. Still, there are sales clerks walking around to help you find what you're looking for.

Next door is the popular **RACHEL'S** dress shop which carries petite and plus sizes next to each other so someone has a sense of humor. After wandering all through the mall, your feet will hurt. This is a good time to buy comfortable shoes at a discount and the best place, LAS Comfort at ST160 Parade.

The bad—and alas often the ugly—is the fact that row upon row carries the same thing at the same price. After a while, especially if you have the strength to cover all 500 shops, you get tired of the same endless low-end jewelry shops, phone accessory items, women's sequined T-shirts, etc. But just when you swear you'll never come back, you find one thing you've been looking for, or you spot something you needed, or you stumble upon an outrageous bargain, and then it's all worthwhile. And next thing you know, you come back again.

JEZEBEL

www.facebook.com/ilovejezebel//Gateway Shopping Center, 1980 E. Sunrise Blvd./Fort Lauderdale 33304 /(954) 761-7881/ OPEN: Mon-Fr. 11-7; Sat.11-8; Sun.12-5.

This fun and funky two-part shop is chock-full-of hip gifts, hilarious cards, stylish candles, unique home décor, vintage jewelry, T-shirts, candles, incense, soap, parasols, and everything in between, like humor books with titles like "How to Get Into Debt." (Many compulsive shoppers don't need any help in doing that.)

There's a small amount of vintage in the front section, for example, old Lucite bags, vintage jewelry, antique hats, and those weird cat's-eye vintage sunglasses that only the brave dare wear today.

"You never know what we'll have," says Mary, the owner. Whatever it is, it's good. They were voted the best boutique shop by *Broward New Times*.

NANNIE'S VINTAGE

www.facebook.com/NanniesVintage// 7880 Wiles Rd/Coral Springs 33067/ (954) 796-2101 / OPEN: Tues.-Sat. 10:30-4

Nannie's offers so many good things for so many people. "We've got the Bling," is their motto, and you can see that bling is their thing. Up front is a lot of vintage, especially handbags and jewelry. In the back there's a whole new world of mostly women's (and a few men's) clothes at double-take prices. But there's more than just vintage clothes here. As you enter you'll see a modern and very unvintagey-looking jewelry store. They not only sell watches (including Rolexes), custom designed rings, and silver charms, but they also do jewelry and watch repair on the premises.

SAWGRASS MILLS OUTLET STORES

www.simon.com/mall/sawgrass-mills; Facebook: Sawgrass Mills //
12801 W. Sunrise Blvd./ Sunrise 33323 / (954) 846-2350 / OPEN:
Mon.–Sat. 10–9:30; Sun.11–8

This wonderful 350-store outlet mall houses the super-posh stores as
well as mid-level shops with plenty of bargains in each and every one
of these places as well as the super expensive ones.

True, some of the merchandise is last year's (who cares?) and some
of it is made especially for malls and outlets (again, who cares), but
you can still find great buys everywhere. It's best to arrive when it
opens and get out by 2 when it gets really crowded—especially on a
holiday or big shopping day.

The mall is divided into colors, making it easy to find something in a
particular section. If you're looking for luxury, the back outdoor
section, The Oasis, has a Nordstrom Rack with clothes from the
department store. (Most Nordstrom Racks have clothes made
especially for them.)

The second luxury area is up front, and the distance is so great you
may even want to repark your car to get there. This Colonnade
section has all the heavy-hitters, like Burberry, St. Johns, Coach,
Barney's Department Store, Tory Burch, Robert Graham, etc. The
Colonnade also has the Neiman Marcus (widely known as Needless
Markup) Last Call store, with genuine merchandise from their store at
greatly reduced prices.

In back of Neimans, where they have the gifts and furniture, is an
exit. If you cross over, you'll stumble upon a great Marshalls. Some
say the best in Broward is in Coral Ridge but this one is terrific, too.
And in the new Century 21 area, you'll find LXR & CO which
carries super-expensive vintage handbags at (still ridiculously
expensive) reduced prices.

SOME MEN LIKE IT HAUTE

www.somemenlikeithaute.com; Facebook: Some Men Like It Haute // 2378 Wilton Dr. / Wilton Manors 33305 / (954) 561- 8650 / OPEN: Tues. Wed. Thurs. 11-2 & 5pm-8 pm; Fri., Sat.12-9; Sun. 12-6

This is the only men's fine fashion consignment shop in Broward County—and one of only two currently in South Florida (See MAN CAVE in the Jupiter/Juno/Tequesta Chapter.)

Behind an upscale storefront, in the heart of Wilton Manors, you'll find this elegant shop selling only new or very gently worn upscale designer shirts, shorts, tee shirts, pants, short sleeve shirts, and plenty of shoes, including sandals, sneakers, slip-ons, loafers and lace-ups, like Ferragamo, Gucci, Cole Haan, Prada and more.

This is the place to get those hard-to-find consigned accessories like men's sunglasses, belts, ties, cufflinks—and even luggage. From Armani to Zegna, they carry a wide variety of designers with many names that you know (and would like to own more of).

VINTAGE DIVERSITY

www.vintagediversity.com; Facebook: Vintage Diversity Inc // 236 W. Prospect Rd. / Fort Lauderdale (Oakland Park) 33309 / (954) 566-7678 OPEN: Tues.-Fri. 12-6; Sat.11-6

The unusual sights and sounds of days gone by provide a delightfully colorful atmosphere from the moment you walk into Vintage Diversity. Unusually large for a vintage shop, the 3,000 square feet is filled with living nostalgia from past eras available for sale or rent. From flapper to funky, and poodle to punky. Everything is clearly marked by size and era.

They have a vast inventory of '20's Flapper & '30's Gangster, '40's Wartime & Hollywood glamor, '50's Poodle skirts and bowling shirts,'60's hippie & Mod GoGo Girl, '70's Rocker or Disco Dancer, '80's Punk Rocker, Valley Girl, Surfer Dude and more. They also rent vintage clothing, costumes, collectibles and props for parties and special occasions, and will outfit you from head to toe. The $125.00 costume rental includes everything from your wig to your shoes, and kids sizes are available for around $45.00.

WORTH REPEATING

www.worthrepeatingfineconsignments.blogspot.com;
Facebook: Worth Repeating // 1732 NE 26th St./ Fort Lauderdale
(Wilton Manors) 33305/ (954) 563–4443/OPEN: Mon.–Sat. 10-5

Worth Repeating Fine Consignments is worth (repeatedly) going to if you're looking for beautiful high-end clothes and accessories. It's in a lovely Colonial-front building, contributing to the feeling that you're going to a fine retail store. Then, when you enter this bright and beautiful shop, you're almost overwhelmed with how much is there and how great it all is. And surprise. The large open "closets" on the far wall contain more St. John than at St. John! Here you can buy their tops, dresses,  pants, and pantsuits in pristine condition at a great price—especially when you consider what these same garments would cost at the "real" place.

This large well-stocked one-room store is unusually full for an upscale consignment so you'll have plenty of great things to go through. Indeed, it's even larger than it looks at first because of a back area to the right that's filled with even more beautiful merchandise.

Women have happily found it worth repeating their visits to Worth Repeating for over 25 years.

"Sweater: garment worn by child when its mother is feeling chilly."

—Ambrose Bierce

꽃 ꠐꠌ

THREE GREAT ANTIQUE MALLS IN BROWARD COUNTY

COOPER CITY ANTIQUE MALL
www.coopercityantiquemall.com; Facebook: Cooper City Antique Mall
// 9800 Grifffin Rd. / Cooper City 33328 / (954) 252-0788 / OPEN:
Mon.-Sat. 10-6; Sun. 12-5

I was destined to like any place named Cooper since that is my maiden
name and they didn't disappoint. From the moment I walked in I felt
like I was in a beautiful new world. "The dealers display their wares,
they don't just toss them in," explained Claudia Cayne, one of the
owners.

Besides the cornucopia of fine quality antiques and collectibles
throughout the 10,000 square feet, they offer design/decorating services,
will help you put together an estate tag sale, buy your gold and silver,
offer an online wish list, have a few artists in residence specializing in
repurposed art, plus so much more. If that's possible.

HILLSBORO ANTIQUE MALL & CAFÉ
www.hillsboroantiquemall.com; Facebook: Hillsboro Antique Mall //
2900 W. Sample Rd. / Pompano Beach 33073 / (954) 571-9988 / OPEN:
Mon.–Fri. 9:30–5; Sat. Sun. 9:30–6. The Hillsboro Antique Mall's 250
dealers (in 35,000 square feet) are looking to appeal to the shoppers at
the flea market next door—who are generally seeking more affordable
bargains—so you can find some good prices. There are six aisles (plus
alcoves) containing a variety of antiques and collectibles, with more of
the latter.

THE SUGAR CHEST ANTIQUE MALL
www.thesugarchestantiquemall.com; Facebook: The Sugar Chest
Antique Mall // 960 N. Federal Hwy. / Pompano Beach 33062 / (954)
942-8601OPEN: Mon.-Fri. 10:30-6; Sat.10-6; Sun.12-6

With 200 booths and 30,000 square feet, the showroom just keeps going
and going and going. You can find something for $5 (not much) or
$5,000 (not much) but most things here cost far far less. There's also
plenty of jewelry here, (including real jewelry in display cases up front),
and paintings, as well as some furniture and home décor. They even do
lamp refurbishing, repair, and rewiring.

꽃 ꠐꠌ

Miami

2ND TIME AROUND

www.2ndtimearound.com; Facebook: 2nd Time Around // 5770
Sunset Drive (72nd St.) / Miami 33143 / (305) 668-9335 / OPEN:
Mon.-Sat. 10-7; Sun. 12-6

This franchise was featured on the Bravo TV reality series on
consignment shops. And bravo to this Miami—and Coconut Grove
one. Could we live without another one? They're in 11 states and
have three in Florida, all carrying contemporary women's clothes &
Accessories at excellent prices. They started 35 years ago with one
boutique and then along came their television series…

COCONUT GROVE SHOP: 3403 Main Highway, (786) 409-2455.
They have the same hours as the Miami one except they open at 11.

NOTE: There's a third **2ND TIME AROUND** in Fort Lauderdale at
1034 Los Olas Boulevard, (954) 763-3586 and this one is open from
11-8 Monday-Saturday.

BACK IN STYLE

www.backinstyle.com; Facebook: Backinstyle.com // 2209 SW 10 St.
/ Miami 33135 / (866) 642-6426 / OPEN: via appointment

This is one of the most pleasant shopping experiences you can have.
But you have to make an appointment to go to this 1920's historic
house in the residential district of Miami. There, you'll find an
amazing collection of vintage designer clothing and dresses from
over 250 designers. By the way, the owner has the largest collection
of vintage Emilio Pucci clothes/accessories in the world. Once in this
lovely four-room house, you'll be welcomed by the charming and
helpful owner, Sheffield, before sifting through an extraordinary
collection of vintage and designer clothing and accessories. One
small room alone is just for furs, and another of clearance items
starting at $10. "We have low overhead so we try to be affordable,"
said Sheffield. Add to that, personable. Just a few reasons why the
Huffington Post said this was one of Miami's best vintage shops.

C. MADELEINE'S

www.cmadeleines.com; Facebook: C Madeleine's //13702 Biscayne Blvd./Miami 33181/ (305) 945-7770/ OPEN: Mon.-Sat. 11-6; Sun. 10-5

Some told me it was a vintage shop. Others called it a super high-end consignment shop for women's clothes. And a gallery. Plus a place  where lots of movie wardrobe people come to dress their stars. It turned out to all be true. And more.

This place, which (im)modestly calls itself "one of the fashion wonders of the world" is an adventure and a destination in itself! It's definitely the best vintage shop in Florida—maybe in the world. And not everything is outrageously priced. "There are deals here and we're here to help you find them," said a saleswoman at this extraordinary shop in North Miami Beach.

Want a $100,000 evening gown from their couture gown department (one of three evening gown sections)? It's here. Want a $28 pair of earrings? Or a $45 leather clutch bag? You'll find them too. You'll even find sales: once a year they have a huge vintage yard sale. Sign up in their guest book or check their Facebook page.

CONSIGN OF THE TIMES

www.consignofthetimes.com; Facebook: Consign of the Times // 1935 West Ave. #05 / Miami Beach 33139 / (305) 535-0811 / OPEN: Mon.-Sat. 10-7; Sun. 12-5

This is the flagship location; the other is in South Miami. A small but elegant shop is very very high end—but there were some hidden treasures too. For example, a Tory Burch orange clutch in the window was $45. But you don't come here for bargains: it's for those on the hunt for luxury goods, especially rare and hard-to-find pieces. Sign up on-line for what is jokingly called their "Lust List" which gives you a list of designers whose clothes you can't live without and they'll e-mail you to tell you when you can start living with them.

SOUTH MIAMI SHOP: There's another **CONSIGN OF THE TIMES** at 6931 Red Road, (305) 667-6675. They're open Mon.-Wed. 10-6; Thurs.-Sat. 10-7; Sun. 12-5. This second small outpost also had a lot of beautiful garments and accessories, although most were still quite pricey. Still, there were some good deals. "We're not as crazy here," said the woman in charge, presumably comparing this shop's prices to the other.

FLY BOUTIQUE VINTAGE

www.flyboutiquevintage.com; Facebook: FlyBoutique // 7235 Biscayne Blvd. / Miami 33138 / (305) 604-8508 / OPEN: Mon.-Fri. Sun. 11-7; closed Sat.

Fly, no walk rapidly to Fly Boutique, because some of the merchandise is out of this world. Located in the MiMo district, they carry a wide range for vintage enthusiasts but it's not limited to clothing accessories, furniture and doodads there. As Zagat said: "You'll never know what you may stumble upon, like artsy lamps, velvet couches, and rotary phones." As one out-of-town vintage shopper said to me when I was there: "I would move to Miami in a heartbeat just to shop at this store regularly! The beaches don't hurt either...."

Still, don't expect thrift store prices because you won't see thrift store merchandise. You will see real vintage and a lot of it is in small sizes, since people were not as ahem, hefty as many are today. Some of what's here is so nice, though, it might make you think about going on a diet...

LINCOLN ROAD OUTDOOR ANTIQUE & COLLECTIBLE MARKET

This antique and collectible show is held in South Beach every second Sunday from October to May from 8-5 between the 800 and 1000 blocks of Lincoln Road. Over 100 booths are filled with small treasures and vintage collectibles including art, jewelry, furniture, clothing and Miami memorabilia.

MIAMI TWICE

www.miamitwice.com; Facebook: Miami Twice // 6562 Bird Rd., (also SW 40th St.) / Miami 33155 / (305) 666-0127 / OPEN: Mon.-Sat. 10-7

If you consider Halloween to be THE major holiday of the year, is this the place for you! They consider themselves to be—and most agree—the "best Halloween and accessories emporium in Miami." They probably don't have a lot of competition on that one, but they do have competition in regular clothing, which frequently beats them on prices. Still, you will find what you won't see elsewhere in this large emporium which carries contemporary clothes, mostly up front, with vintage further in the back. And, of course, Halloween items in the month of October.

SECOND SHOWING

www.secondshowingmiami.com // 8191 SW 117th St. / Miami 33156 (305) 971-0747 / OPEN: Mon.-Wed. 10-6; Thurs. 10-7:30; Fri. Sat. 10-6; Sun. 12-5

This is exactly the kind of consignment shop I love—and you will too It's a large, rectangular-shaped space, with a double-rack of clothes on each side and lots of goodies in the middle. Nothing here is more than one to two years old and it's all in perfect condition. There are plenty of accessories, and to give you an idea of its scope, shoes are in three different sections! Finally, there's plenty of sale merchandise around. Lots (most, really) of the items before a reduction were under $100. And there was even a $10 rack.

They've been around since 1975 and carry everything from vintage to contemporary, to jeans for teens, to elegant gowns for grownups. It's easy to find because it's in the north end of the Suniland (Whole Foods) Shopping Center, by the bank. You can bank on this place.

THE CONSIGNMENT BAR

www.consignmentbar.com; Facebook: The Consignment Bar // 5580 NE 4th Ct. #4A / Miami 33137 / (305) 751-9996 / OPEN: Mon.-Sat. 12-7; Sun. 12-5

Are you "Gaga for Gucci? Loco for Coco?" asks Maria Tettamanti, who is Miami's premier fashion and shopping writer, (see www.thewordygirl.com). She says that The Consignment Bar is where to get "your high-fashion fix" with their "fancy schmancy brands but not their price tags."

This "luxury consignment boutique" as they call themselves is definitely a great place for the style seekers and fashion savvy. It's located on the upper east side of Biscayne Boulevard, less than five minutes from Miami's Design District at the 55th Street Station. Once you get there, you'll become part a luxurious environment, making the experience of shopping for upscale items so delightful.

THE FASHIONISTA CONSIGNMENT BOUTIQUE

www.thefashionistaboutique.com; Facebook: The Fashionista Consignment Boutique // 3135 Commodore Plaza / Coconut Grove 33133 / (305) 443-4331 / OPEN: Mon.-Sat. 11-5

This swanky and chic but very small very high-end fashion boutique in the heart of Coconut Grove off Grand Avenue has big-name labels at big buck prices. Run by a mother and daughter who know that there are bargainistas as well as fashionistas, they offer an enticing reduced rack along with the gorgeous but almost faint-prices of the rest of the garments.

THE RABBIT HOLE

www.shoprabbithole.com; Facebook: The Rabbit Hole; Instagram: shoprabbithole// 17032 W. Dixie Hwy. / North Miami Beach 33160 / (305) 705-2343 / OPEN: Tues.-Sat. 12-8; Sun 2-6

"Bargain Bunnies" will find more here than in most comparable vintage shops. Which is not to say it's inexpensive but that there are some good deals. Indeed, *New Times* in 2011 voted this the best second-hand store in Miami when it was only a year old.

They're still filled with hand-picked items sourced from all over the world, and there are some unique garments and accessories from the '50's to the '90's. Plus something very unusual for a resale shop: you can return items (if the tag is still on it) for a week after you've purchased it. So hop on down....

THIS 'N THAT SHOP

Facebook: This 'N That Shop // 3155 Commodore Plaza / Coconut Grove 33133 / (305) 448-2114 / OPEN: Tues.-Sat.10-4:30

You wouldn't expect to stumble upon a thrift shop in high-end Coconut Grove, but there is it, a few doors down from **THE FASHIONISTA** (see above). But this is a "quality thrift shop" that doesn't sell just about anything as a regular thrift does. Even so, the clothes/accessories were unexciting. But there was plenty else to choose from in this two-room shop. For example, a magnificent 4-piece set of china in perfect condition in a Nordstrom box was $22.50.

TWICE

www.twiceconsign.com; Facebook: Twice Consignment // 4040 Red Road. / Miami 33155 / (305) 665-7620 / OPEN: Tues.-Sat. 11-5; Sun. 12-4

Don't confuse Twice with **MIAMI TWICE** since that is a vintage shop which becomes a Halloween shop in October. This contemporary clothing shop's closest holiday would be "Christmas" or "Christmas in July" since you'll find plenty to please you here. Actually, there is a little vintage but mostly it's (moderate to upscale) contemporary clothes and jewelry plus housewares that fill the place.

ഇൗരു

Hail to the Veep

You find strange bargains in resale shops, as one man learned last year after purchasing a Brooks Brothers shirt for $1 in his local resale shop. That would have been good enough. But when he unrolled the sleeves, cufflinks fell out. And they were gold. Making it even more valuable, they were inscribed as well: *United States Senator Joseph H. Biden Jr.* It appeared that the Vice President (or his wife) had donated his shirt to a thrift shop, forgetting that his cufflinks were still in it.

BARGAIN SAVING TIP: MALLS VS. ANTIQUE SHOPS

Price-conscious shoppers are more likely to find a bargain in a mall than in a regular antique store. In a mall, dealers may offer lower prices because the competition is right there. If it's too expensive, or not quite what someone wants, he or she can easily move on to another booth. In addition, sadly, a few exhibitors are always going out of business, and you can find some bargains in their booths.

PART III
ANTIQUES

NORTHWOOD—A MINI ANTIQUE ROW

Whether you call it "North South Beach" or "Mini Antique Row," this charming three-block area in West Palm Beach is sprinkled with a collection of unusual shops, artsy windows, antiques, collectibles and restaurants.

You'll find this section north of downtown West Palm Beach, but once you get there don't go far past the shopping area. It borders Riviera Beach. Enough said. But you'll be perfectly safe (and happy!) wandering down this European-style street. Especially since what you'll find in Northwood usually costs far less than at most antique shops elsewhere. Indeed, some of these stores were originally located on Dixie's more expensive Antique Row before settling here.

The atmosphere here is much more casual; the owner of one gallery came out to greet a customer barefoot. They also occasionally have wine tastings street-side artists, and live entertainment.

Here, alphabetically, are the top antique, vintage and consignment shops in Northwood.

ABOUT DETAILS: 528 24th St. / (561) 512-5674 /OPEN: By appointment. Upholstery shop for furniture, fabrics, window treatments, and more.

CHURCHILL GALLERIES: www.churchillgalleries.com; www.facebook.com/churchillgalleries //412 Northwood Rd./(561) 835-4774/ OPEN: Wed.-Sat., 11-5. Antiques, estate furnishings, mirrors, lamps, chandeliers, decorative accessories, and selected artwork. The main gallery is on Antique Row at 3628 Dixie Highway, and they also have a shop in Tinson Antique Galleries at 544 Northwood Road.

DAY BY DAY SHOPPE: www.daybydaynorthwood.com // 511B Northwood Rd. / (561) 623-9353. Eclectic mix of unique home furnishings, gifts, and more.

D'S CLOSET: 408 Northwood Rd. / (561) 249-0578 / OPEN: Tues.-Fri. 11-6; Sat. 12-7. A contemporary boutique carrying high-end clothing.

DIANE'S BOUTIQUE: Facebook: Diane's Boutique // 515 ½ Northwood Rd. / (561) 317- 6091 / OPEN: Don't ask Diane when her consignment clothes & accessories shop is open, because she doesn't answer. Inside the tiny shop are three rows of shoes, handbags, and separates. Alas, the prices are often harder to find than the hours, and there's so much clothes that it's hard to get around.

DANIELLE EMON BOUTIQUE:
www.DanielleEmon.com; Facebook: Danielle Emon Boutique // 2325 Spruce Ave. / (561) 231-0743 / OPEN: Tues.-Fri. 11-7 and by appointment. A block from Northwood Road is this fashion house carrying clothing, jewelry, and accessories.

NORTHWOOD ANTIQUES & DESIGN:
Facebook: Northwood Antiques & Design Palm Beach // 420 Northwood Rd. / (561) 588-0129 / OPEN: Mon.-Sat. 10-5 and some evenings. Featuring antiques, estates, rugs, palm trees, old trains, and two large white Foo dogs outside who welcome you inside.

NORTHWOOD GLASS ART AND GIFTS:
www.northwoodglasart.com; Facebook: Northwood Glass Art // 524 Northwood Rd. / (561) 329-4280 / OPEN: Tues.-Sat. 10:30-5. This has always been one of the loveliest shops on the street, filled with beautiful glass jewelry, bracelets, frames, plates, memory boxes, and a small amount of consigned jewelry and woodworking pieces. Best of all, they'll help you make your own glass art and mosaics in their

regular classes. This place has attractive merchandise and a lovely ambiance.

SOMETHING LIVELY: www.somethinglively.com // 540 Northwood Rd. / (561) 319-3151 / OPEN: Mon.-Fri. 10-30-4; Sat. 11-4; Sun. By appointment. Something Lively really deserves its name because there's always something lively going on here. This mini antique mall includes the Tinson Antique Galleries (antiques & art), art studios, the Palm Beach Restoration Studios (specializing in restoring art, porcelain, and marble) and more. David is always doing something lively, like getting involved with the ARTnight Out the last Friday of each month, (6-9 PM), the art walk through the gallery on the 2nd Saturday (6-9) and the Food Track Rally on the 3rd Wednesday (6-9) of the month.

THE PAINTED MERMAID:

www.thepaintedmermaidwpb.com; Facebook: The Painted Mermaid // 437 Northwood Rd. / (561) 328-9859 / OPEN: Tues.-Sat. 9-6. They custom paint outdoor and indoor furniture to give it a one-of-a-kind look that matches the rest of your décor.

THE PURPLE BOUGAN-VILLA:

www.thepurplebouganvilla.com; Facebook: The Purple Bougan-Villa // 423 Northwood Rd. / (561) 246-1777 / OPEN: Mon.-Sat. 12-5. They carry lots of colorful and unique home décor, unusual vintage and antique furnishings, gifts, and a lovely selection of handbags, jewelry and scarves from France & Italy.

TINSON ANTIQUES GALLERIES: 538- 544 Northwood Rd. / (561) 319-351. Over 12,000 square feet and seven showrooms of fine art, antiques. They also do appraisals, estate liquidation sales and more. In business since 1965.

LOOK WHAT I FOUND!

I became a fan of **SCOTT SIMMONS** when he was writing his *Palm Beach Post* antique column. Now he's editor at *Florida Weekly,* and his transplanted column is titled "Look What I Found." It runs every Thursday and you can also read it at www.scottsimmonsantiques.com.

In addition, he pens a "Collector's Corner," where you can learn everything about the care, collection, and sale of antiques, like how to keep silver shiny (don't over clean it). Here are more tips.

- Dealers will only give you 20-30% of what they think an item is worth because they have to pay for space to display it, insurance, etc. Most consignment shops will give you 50%.

- Don't bring items to a dealer to sell in the summertime. Business will be down and it will sit on a shelf after Easter/Passover/Mother's Day. Then, it's more likely to be marked down, and you will get less on your end, too.

- If you consign something for a certain period of time, mark on your calendar when you can reclaim it if it isn't sold.

- The value of antiques and your ability to sell them may depend on where you live. For example, a formal place setting may be worth nothing in Florida but be of value up north, where people still set formal tables.

- Old figurines that were made in press molds will have one or two small holes punched into the clay to allow air to escape. Newer pieces will have dime-size or larger holes in the bottom.

- Gold decoration on antique pieces should be slightly dull because it tarnishes over time.

- Use your treasures—don't keep them hidden away in a china cabinet. It only takes an extra few minutes to hand wash instead of machine washing something.

SIXTEEN DON'T-MISS ANTIQUE SHOPS IN ANTIQUE ROW

There is a sameness about many of the shops along West Palm Beach's Antique Row, an area ranging from approximately 3900 South Dixie Highway to 3416. Going north, here are a few shops, on Dixie that carries unique items. (Note that many don't open until 11 or 12 noon and are not open on Sundays.)

FAUX FLOWERS: **THE FLORAL EMPORIUM** has five rooms filled with gorgeous faux floral arrangements and floral decorating décor, ranging in price from a few dollars to thousands. Just walking in and looking around is a delight, especially at Christmastime. They also have special sales after the holiday season. / www.floralemporiumonline.com / 3900 S. Dixie Hwy. / (562) 659-9888

GARDEN FURNITURE: **AUTHENTIC PROVENCE** is filled indoors and outdoors (in their "Secret Garden") with French and Italian garden antiques & furnishings, including urns, spouts, and planters. / www.authenticprovence.com / 3735 S. Dixie Hwy. / (561) 805-9555

ORIENTAL RUGS: **DIAMOND ANTIQUE ORIENTAL RUGS** sells handmade vintage and antique rugs, wall hangings, and cushion covers from Turkey, Iran, and Russia. www.diamondantiqueorientalrugs.com / 3720 S. Dixie Hwy. / (561) 650-7333

LIGHTING: If you're looking for lamps, chandeliers, lampshades, or lamp repair or rewriting, try **HEATH & COMPANY** at 3707 S. Dixie Hwy (561) 833-0880. And while you're at that mall, pop into **CASHMERE BUFFALO** next door. Simply from the name of this place (what the heck is a cashmere buffalo?) you know you're going to find unusual things. Or as they say, "textures & inspirations, little luxuries, and objects of desire."

TABLE TOPS: **DEVONIA,** Antiques for Dining, is a beautiful shop (in the mall mentioned above), filled with fine tableware, such as antique porcelain, glass, plates, cups, saucers, and centerpieces. (They also have a booth at Bergdorf Goodman's in NY**.) /** www.devonia-antiques.com / 3703A S. Dixie Hwy. / (561) 429-8566

HORSES: You don't have to go all the way to Wellington to find horse-related décor. Neigh, I mean no, you can go to the 2600 square-foot spectacular ARC gallery at 3636 S. Dixie Hwy. In the back is a small booth by **GRAY FADDEN**, who has such artifacts as vintage horse figurines, brass horse statues, and carved wooden horses. /www.chairish.com/shop/iaun2g / 3636 S. Dixie Hwy. / (203) 912-5837

VINTAGE CLOTHING: **PALM BEACH VINTAGE** calls itself "A Palm Beach secret since 1978" and carries vintage couture and designer clothes and accessories in one large room. Owner Louise Pinson explained that: "My vintage is one-of-a-kind designer and renegade, one season wunderkind, from the 1800's through the 1980's and a little later, and occasionally something sneaks in from Chanel or Dior, or who knows who."/ www.palmbeachvintage.com / 3623 S. Dixie Hwy. (561) 718-4075.

Another high-end vintage shop is on the second floor of **ARC** (Antique Row Consignments) at 3636 S Dixie. There, you'll find two boutiques of vintage clothing and accessories run by **LIZ LIPPMAN**. The second "boutique" area is the higher-end vintage, although the first one is pretty high too.

NOTE: Directly across from ARC and Lippman's place above is a tiny mall with a very popular restaurant: **BELLE & MAXWELL'S** at 3700 South Dixie. It's great for lunch—especially their famous carrot cake!

VINTAGE JEWELRY: If you love eye-popping vintage jewelry, stop at **D. BRETT BENSON** on Antique Row, or visit his popular booth usually near the entrance in the second room at the Florida Fairgrounds Antique show. (See West Palm Beach & Wellington chapter.) At both places, you'll find his gorgeous vintage American and European couture and designer costume jewelry. /www.dbrettbensoninc.com/ 3616 S. Dixie Hwy. / (561) 512-1389

A TURQUOISE TURTLE: No, you won't find an actual turquoise turtle here at the oddly-named **TURQUOISE TURTLE** but you'll find just about everything else in a warm, friendly shop whose eclectic items often have a touch of the Caribbean. (Hence the "turquoise.") They have everything from vintage clothing to unique items for interiors, and they also do interiors. / www.turquoise-turtle.com / 3609 S. Dixie Hwy. / (561) 309-9099

AFRICAN ART: **OUT OF AFRICA ART SHOP** sells artwork and artifacts from Africa, including yarn paintings, Moroccan furniture, jewelry, masks, dolls, drums, wood carvings, decorative items, and other unusual items. / www.outofafricaartshop.com / 3606 S. Dixie Hwy., #130 / (561) 676-9222

BALLROOM GOWNS: Who better to choose ballroom gowns than someone who has worn them herself? Peggy Middleton, a former ice skater, has a shop in the back of **TIMELESS ANTIQUES** carrying ballroom gowns and consignment pieces. When you do meet her, don't expect her to be all dolled up in one of her gowns. "I don't want to look better than my clients," she said. / 3512 S. Dixie Hwy. / (561) 655-3235. By appointment.

PEACHY BEACHY: **COASTAL GIRLS** is a pleasant surprise because it's all beachy-type contemporary clothes, accessories, and gifts—and the prices are considerably less than at most places along the avenue. / Facebook: Coastal Girls Co. / 3508 S. Dixie Hwy. / (561) 619-5389

SURPRISE: There's a surprise at 3415 South Dixie in this two-story 20,000-square-foot gallery and it isn't just how beautiful (and expensive) the 18th and 19th century French Italian and continental antiques are at **CEDRIC DU PONT GALLERIES**. It's that the man who sometimes greets you a few days a week is Tony Senecal, Donald Trump's (controversial) former butler, whom you may have read about in the news. **NOTE**: It's worth coming to a group of design dealers at 2800 S. Dixie Highway who call themselves the "Iconic Snob" gallery, not just for the attractiveness of what they offer, but when someone asks you where you went on Antique Row, you can honestly say "Oh, I stopped by at that snob place..." **For more antique shops, go to** www.westpalmbeachantiques.com for maps and descriptions of these and other places.

In addition, there's the monthly Antiques & Collectibles Show at the South Florida Fairgrounds (see West Palm Beach/Wellington chapter). And don't forget the two large antique malls in nearby Lake Worth: **All Good Things** and **BKG Galleries**. (See Lake Worth chapter). Plus, antiques are sold at many of the other shops in this book.

HOW NOT TO GET CONNED WHEN BUYING "ANTIQUES"

True story. A woman went to appraise an antique Greek vase she had purchased for $1500. It turned out to be a fancy $10 jar for olive oil that had been "aged."

1) Looking used or "old" is not enough. As they said in *Antiquing for Dummies*: "You can hire one hundred people to trample a new Oriental rug and give it that worn in look." Linens may be soaked in tea to make them look aged, or furniture might be beaten with a chain to make it look used and weathered.

2) If a piece of jewelry is glued into the setting with no prongs holding it in, it's probably costume jewelry with no value.

3) Bring a small magnet with you to test if gold is real. Gold is not magnetic, so if the item sticks to the magnet, it's not real. Generally gold and silver are heavier than their fake counterparts like brass and pewter.

4) When having a piece appraised, pay per piece, not a percentage of its worth. Otherwise, an appraiser may increase its value to get a greater percentage.

5) Ask for a very detailed receipt of the item in case there's a problem later.

6) Buy from a collector of the item you're buying. They're more likely to care about what they sell and can help you determine if it's the real deal.

7) Check the internet. If there is a lot of the item, it probably isn't valuable.

8) Smell it. If the wood has been painted or something added, you can often smell it.

9) The general rule is that old rusts brown, new rusts orange, eBay warned.

PART IV
THRIFT SHOPS

८১০৫৪
21 THRIFT SHOPS WITH SUPER BARGAINS AND ROCK BOTTOM PRICES

Remember the difference between a thrift and a consignment shop. People donate to thrifts (and "sell" to consignments) so the merchandise is usually not as good at thrifts but the prices are generally much lower.

A few "quality" thrift shops (like **NEARLY NEW** in West Palm Beach and **CHURCH MOUSE** in Palm Beach) are selective about what they accept. You'll find them listed earlier in the chapters of the towns they're in.

The following places are generally less selective, but you can still snag some very good bargains in them. It's all a matter of luck and timing.

(WPB) ABUSED WOMEN'S THRIFT BOUTIQUE:

This is a large, dark, and heavily stocked thrift shop, but there's something depressing about it. They claim that good consignment/thrift shops regularly donate their name brand clothing to them, but a few of my checks have never turned up anything worth buying. They do carry a few things most thrifts don't, for example, food at the back of the big large main room, plus a lot of well-priced linens in the smaller back room. There are even a few good items behind the cash register, but those aren't the prices you'll see elsewhere and are not enough to warrant a trip. 7110 S. Dixie Hwy. / West Palm Beach/(561) 586-1888 OPEN: Mon. 12-3; Tues.-Sat. 11-4

(JUNO) **ADOPT A CAT RESALE STORE:** Here's something to purr about. If you're a cat lover despairing over the loss of the Adopt a Cat Thrift Shop in Lake Park, they didn't go out of business but moved to Juno. They're now in the same mall as HOSPICE: RESALE SHOP NORTH and LADIES CLOSET. Adopt a Cat is filled, and I mean filled, with clothes, housewares, a bit of furniture, knick-knacks and an occasional (real) cat or two. (Not for sale.) There's probably nothing you would want there, but you might want to purchase something anyway since this thrift supports the 80 cats in their no-kill shelter. www.adoptacatfoundation.org/thrift-store/thriftstore.html / 889 Donald Ross Rd. / Juno Beach / (561) 848-4911 / OPEN: Mon.-Sat. 10-5:30

(GREENACRES)**BLESSINGS AND BARGAINS THRIFT STORE:** Once in there, you'll find long racks of thrifty clothes, clean but not very new looking. Still, there are some occasional finds. For example, a beautiful unworn beaded wedding gown with a matching purse and a long tulle train for $99 was there during a recent check. Mostly, you'll find men and women's apparel for a few bucks—including a small section of men's plus sizes, something you don't see often. That, plus children's clothes and books, and golf clubs for $2 are available in this large clean shop that benefits Faith United Methodist Church in Boynton. Facebook: Blessings & Bargains / 4755 N. Congress Ave. / Boynton Beach / (561) 296-9935 / OPEN: Tues.-Sat. 10-5

(BOCA) **COMMUNITY FAMILY THRIFT STORE:** They claim to be the largest used furniture warehouse in South Florida. They're filled with a huge selection of merchandise, from gently-used household appliances and furniture to clothes and accessories. Truckloads of donated products arrive daily for consumers and wholesalers, and they always have specials.

They've been open in the same location since 1990. www.communityfamilythrift.com / 23269 S. State Rd., 7 / Boca Raton / (561) 487-7118 / OPEN: Mon.-Sat. 9-6; Sun. 11-4

(BOCA) FAMILY SAFE HAVEN THRIFT STORE & BOUTIQUE:

If you happen to be at the two better thrift shops at Plum Park across the street (LEVIS JCC & HOSPICE—see Boca chapter) you'll spot this one situated in the strip mall across from Plum Park. Sometimes there are a few better garments for women and men up front and to the right as you enter. You can skip the rest of the clothes, especially the used underwear in bins (ugh) near the counter.

In back of the counter and around it, you'll occasionally turn up some good small appliances and computer-related products. A recent check turned up a great scanner at an excellent price—but the instructions were entirely in Spanish. Even if you speak a smattering of the language, could you really set up a complicated piece of equipment using what may be your second language?

The second room to the left also leaves much to be desired in clothing, but there are some kitchen, household items, and appliances. You might even find something at a good price. Hopefully in English. www.familysafehaveninc.org / 146 NW 20th St. / Boca Raton / (561) 368-3339 / OPEN: Mon.-Fri. 10:30 -5:30; Sat. 10-6.

(JUPITER) FURRY FRIENDS PICK OF THE LITTER BOUTIQUE & THRIFT STORE:

www.furryfriendsadoption.org/#!-thrift-shop/iemwe/
615 W. Indiantown Rd. / (561) 529-4075; Tues.-Fri. 10-5; Sat. 10-4.

Since the money you spend here goes to a good cause (Humane Society of Greater Jupiter/Tequesta) drop by if you're next door at **CONSIGN-IT.** To be honest, I was extremely disappointed with what I saw when I checked out Furry Friends, and the attractive furniture/décor on their Facebook page was not in sight during my visit. But maybe it was a bad day. Still, don't get your expectations up too high.

(WPB) HOSPICE: RESALE SHOP CENTRAL:

There are three Hospice resale shops now, which is too bad, because too much merchandise spread out into many stores means fewer bargains in any one of them. The neighborhood a thrift is in is very important, since those sorting the merchandise generally send the better items to the more affluent neighborhoods. That's why the hospices in Boca and

Juno tends to carry the better goods. (See chapters on Jupiter/Juno and Boca.) This one, which moved from an even worse neighborhood on Military Trail, is now in the WPB Merchandise Mart. It's all one large room, divided in two, one for furniture/ home decor and the other for clothes. Don't expect too much and you won't be disappointed. www.hpbcf.org/ 4833 Okeechobee Blvd. / West Palm Beach / (561) 681-6511 OPEN: Mon.-Sat. 10-5.

NEARBY SHOP: **A WALMART SUPERCENTER** is one-half a mile away at 4375 Belvedere Rd., and the **GOODWILL WEST PALM BEACH CLEARANCE CENTER** is nearby at 1897 Old Okeechobee Road.

(WPB–NORTHWOOD) **MELANIE'S REAL THRIFT & THINGS:** I was underwhelmed by either of the two small rooms here on my one visit. Still, it's only a block from the tonier Northwood shops (See Part III Antique Section) and it's next to a terrific Thai restaurant, Malakor, at 425 25th Street. So if you're in the neighborhood... 413 25th St. / West Palm Beach / (561) 856-558 / OPEN: Mon.-Thurs. 10:30-5:30; Fri. Sat. 10:30-9:30, but closed from 12:30-3:30.

(WPB) **NOAH'S ARK HELPING PETS INC.** Remember Janice from the defunct Peggy Adams Animal Rescue League Thrift Shop? When they closed, she moved nearby and started her own animal charity thrift shop that's heavy on...well, everything. Especially furniture and home décor. The price point is good, and you might snag a bargain. For example, a pair of 30-year-old vintage Christian Dior glasses (only slightly scratched) were $65. Most of the merchandise is much cheaper and the money goes to a good cause. Plus, she'll negotiate. Park at the PNC bank on the corner of nearby Parker Avenue. www.noahsarkhelpingpets.com; Facebook: Noah's Ark Helping Pets Inc. / 824 Belvedere Rd. / West Palm Beach / (561) 833-8131/ OPEN: Mon.-Sat. 9-6; Sun. 12-4.

(PALM BEACH GARDENS) **OH YEAH THRIFT SHOP:** Where on earth did this place get that name? The owners must have been struggling for a name, came up with one, and said "Oh yeah, that's it," But they forgot the name they had just come up with, so they just named it "Oh Yeah." Or maybe they mean "Oh yeah, let's go there." Who knows. It's certainly different. The shop.... not so much. Men, women & children's apparel and a bit of "boutique" clothes. Household items are in the middle room. The room to the right has furniture. Tuesday is up to 50% off for veterans; Every day is 25% off for seniors (55+). 8091 N. Military Trail / Palm Beach Gardens / (561) 799-4870 / OPEN: Mon.-Sat. 10-7.

SHOPS NEARBY: GOODWILL PALM BEACH GARDENS BOUTIQUE at 4224 North Lake Blvd.

(WEST PALM BEACH) **ONE MORE TIME! THRIFT SHOP AND COFFEE BAR:** Would you like to go to a thrift shop where their boutique items are occasionally donated by rich Palm Beach women? Then come on over to South Dixie's One More Time, which supports an important charity: The Lord's Place, which helps the homeless in this county. One More Time carries some budget clothes and miscellaneous household goods and everything is easy to find because it's in separate areas. They have a lot of Christmas goodies and gifts in season, and highly unusual: they have a separate electronics room, which includes TV sets, DVDs and more. www.thelordsplace.org / 7600 S. Dixie Hwy. / West Palm Beach / (561) 494-0125 #6 / OPEN: Mon.-Sat. 9-5.

(LAKE WORTH) **PBHC THRIFT STORE:** This large three-room thrift can be a bit hard to find, but the substantial boutique clothing section in the front makes it worth scouting out. In addition, there are often good finds in housewares and decorative accessories up front. The second room, the budget area, is typical low-priced thrift with everything reduced 50% if it's here a second month. The 3rd small back room has books, videos, and sometimes more unusual items. www.pbhab.com/main/thriftstore / Palm Beach Habilitation Center Campus / 4522 S. Congress Ave. / Lake Worth / (561) 967-5993 / OPEN: Mon.-Sat. 9-4.

(W.PALM-NORTHWOOD)**RECOVERY   RESALE THRIFT:** The dreadful looking racks outside this Northwood thrift shop may keep you from going in but just ignore them. This bright new clean-looking five-room thrift shop has clothing, furniture, shoes, and lots of men's and children's clothes. Alas, the boutique was the only discordant note, since the garments (including two Lillys) were overpriced for a thrift store. But other than that... it's worth a look-see, and the money you spend helps those with addiction—but not those with a shopping addiction! Facebook: Recovery Resale Thrift / 2417 Spruce Ave. / West Palm Beach (Northwood) / (561) 463-HEAL / OPEN: Tues-Fri. 11-6; Sat. 11-4.

(W.PALM BEACH) **SALVATION ARMY ON MILITARY TRAIL:** While I have been a supporter of the Salvation Army, I have never been a supporter of their thrift shops. I have friends who swear by them but usually, I swear at them for having wasted my time by going in one. Several months ago, however, I received the following e-mail from a reader of my previous shopping book about the Salvation Army by the airport. She started by saying that she too had usually been unimpressed by their offerings. "A couple of months ago we saw a change in the display of clothing and furniture and then a complete do-over ... the once dust-filled 'Vintage Room' is now a place for the hardcore thrift shopper to use their imagination." Whatever that means. www.salvationarmyflorida.org / 655 N. Military Trail / (561) 683-3513 / OPEN: Mon.-Sat. 10-6.

(LAKE WORTH) **SALVATION ARMY SUPERSTORE:** The Salvation Army shops have been called "The Saks Fifth Avenue for the tightwad set." Many have found bargains, especially on Wacky Wednesdays when they give 50% off for seniors, teachers, and veterans. Nice. Whatever you buy, it'll be helping some organization that really needs the money. www.salvationarmyflorida.org/4001 Kirk Rd. / Lake Worth / (561) 642-1927 / OPEN: Mon. -Fri. 9-5; Sat. 9-6.

(LAKE PARK) **ST. MARK'S THRIFT SHOP** is a pretty decent thrift with three large heavily-stocked rooms. Two are for furniture, chandeliers, lamps, an occasional piano, electronics, books, glassware, kitchenware, children's clothes, CDs, and movies.

The front section in the first room contains clothing racks that have some minor name brands, a jeans rack, miscellaneous clothes (including men's), purses, pictures, and shoes. Lots and lots of shoes. Up front, though, there are a couple of racks of better (not great) clothing, where you might snag—(as I did) an Alberto Makali blouse which runs a couple of hundred at Nordstrom for $5. They're only open Wednesday through Saturday from 10-4. There's no tax because it's affiliated with a church. http://church.stmarkspbg.org/pages/thrift-shop; www.facebook.com/stmarksthriftshop / 208 US Hwy. 1/ Lake Park / (561) 863-8516.

(LAKE WORTH, JUPITER & TEQUESTA) **ST. VINCENT de PAUL:** They carry furniture, home goods, and clothing. "Vincentians," as their volunteers are called, claim to have helped 14 million people last year through visits to homes, prisons, and hospitals. The charity collects money through their donations and thrift shops. They currently have two thrifts in Palm Beach County: one is at 3757 S. Military Trail in Lake Worth, (561) 469-7922. The other is at 250 W. Indiantown Road in Jupiter 561) 401-9585 OPEN: Lake Worth is Mon.-Fri. 10-6; Sat. 9-5; Jupiter is Mon.-Fri. 10-4; Sat. 9-3.

(LAKE WORTH) **SUNRISE EMPORIUM:** There are some interesting things there, although it used to be called Sunrise Flea Market, and it still is that. The clothes were stylish but not in good condition so forget those. But in the front rooms were also incredible deals on some good shoes ($2.99 a pair) and odd things someone might just want, like a real replica of the Taj Mahal or Korean plates. Well, someone might want them and there they were. That's what thrifting is all about. Discovering something you didn't know you wanted or needed. In the back is a room with electronics and mostly men's clothes, and behind that some forgettable furniture that even so could make some home very happy, especially at that price. Check them out on the web or Facebook. www.sunriseemporium.net; Facebook: Sunrise Emporium Thrift Store 1101 N. Dixie Hwy./ Lake Worth 33460 / (561) 588 - 2898 OPEN: Mon.-Sat. 10-6; Sun. 10-5.

(LAKE PARK) **THE GIVE THRIFT BOUTIQUE:** The Give may relocate to Jupiter but you should look up their new address if they're gone. I'm not recommending them because of the mostly ordinary merchandise in poor condition, but because the owner, Donatella, started this thrift shop after her 11-year-old son died of pancreatic cancer. She promises that whatever money she makes there that doesn't go to rent and utilities goes to help other children with cancer. Prices are very inexpensive, like $4 and $5 for men's & women's shirts, but you're there more to help the cause than to find any bargains. www.thegive1111.com / 1263 10th Street, Clayton Sq. / Lake Park / (561) 842-4483 / OPEN: Mon.-Fri. 10-4:30; Sat.10-3.

(WEST PALM BEACH) **UPSCALE RESALE:** Despite their name, you won't find much that's upscale here, but you will find a few nice things at low prices. They carry a little bit of everything—but don't even look at the clothes. www.upscaleresalewpb.com / 6230 S. Dixie Hwy. / West Palm Beach / (561) 355-5559.

ഇൽൽ

HOW TO SPOT A GOOD THRIFT SHOP

How do you tell if a garment you want to buy is, well, too thrifty? You look at the label to see how worn it is; you look at the pockets to see how stretched it is; and you take a sniff to see how smelly it is.

Says Dan Demicell, a top resale marketing consultant, "When you walk into a thrift shop, it shouldn't smell like one. When you look around it shouldn't look like one. It should be clean, orderly and what you buy should be worth what you pay for it," he stressed.

ഇൽ

PART V

SPECIAL SHOPPING SECTION

CONSIGNMENT CLOTHING FOR MEN

Why aren't there more men's consignment clothing shops? That was explained by Dina Capehart, who owns **DINA C'S FAB & FUNKY** women's consignment/vintage shop in West Palm Beach. "After years of hearing men ask where they can shop consignment, I opened a men's consignment boutique next door to my shop. Unfortunately, I discovered that even though men also like to shop for second-hand designer goods, they DO NOT PART WITH THEM. I had a demand for the items but found that men will resole their shoes 10 times rather than consign them. They hold onto their clothing 'til death do they part' with them."

As a result, there are only two high-end clothing consignment stores left that are now exclusively for men: **MAN CAVE** in Tequesta and **SOME MEN LIKE IT HAUTE** in Broward County.

There are also three women's consignment shops that include a nice selection of men's clothes: **CONSIGNED COUTURE** (North Palm Beach) **FASHION EXCHANGE** (Lake Worth) and **PARADISE LOST** (Palm Beach).

Many thrift shops also carry men's as well as women's clothes. The better ones are **CHURCH MOUSE** (Palm Beach), **HOSPICE BY THE SEA** (Boca Raton), **JCC LEVIS** (Boca Raton), **NEARLY NEW** (West Palm Beach), **ONE MORE TIME** (West Palm Beach), **TRI-COUNTY HUMANE** (Boca Raton), and **WORLD THRIFT** (Lake Worth). You can find descriptions of them in the town chapters and in Part IV, the Thrift Shop section.

CHILDREN'S RESALE SHOPS—WHERE ARE

THEY? A few years ago there were probably a dozen children's consignment shops sprinkled throughout the county. It almost seemed as if anyone who had a child and wanted to start a business thought an easy choice would be to open a children's consignment store.

The problem was that many of them had never run a consignment shop before and didn't know how to do it. Many also didn't computerize, a necessity for consignment shops because the owner has to handle a large numbers of individual consigners and keep track of what was sold and who gets what payment for it.

In addition, many owners thought they could stay home with their children and hire someone else to run their shops. But some employees ran off with their shops, or at least the money.

Almost all of them went out of business. Now, to find children's clothes, you pretty much have to go a thrift shop—and many people don't want to buy heavily used clothes and half-broken toys for their kids.

Fortunately, there are still a few good children's consignment shops left: **CASSIE & JAMES BOUTIQUE** in Palm Beach (Susan sells adult consignment clothing & accessories as well), **FOREVER YOUNG** in Tequesta, **RED BALLOON's** Forest Hill Shop in West Palm Beach, the new **TWINKLE ROCK** in North Palm Beach, and **WILL & EMMA'S CLOSET** in Boca Raton.

There are also a few retail shops that have outlets with children's clothes: **ARISTOKIDS OUTPOST** (West Palm Beach), and **SNAPPY TURTLE OUTLET** (Delray).

THAT'S JUST PEACHY! WHERE TO BUY BEACHY, COASTAL & COTTAGE, SHABBY CHIC, REFURBISHED (UPCYCLED) OR FLORIDA FURNISHINGS

If you don't know whether you like shabby chic because you don't know what it is, the owner and creator of **SHE'S SO SHABBY**, Jodi, describes it as "grandma's furniture painted for today's shabby style."

What you'll find at these shops are repurposed, recycled, reloved, and reshabbified items. **ALL GOOD THINGS** (Lake Worth), **COASTAL MARKETPLACE** (Lake Park), **FUNKY CRAB** (Palm Beach Gardens), **SHE'S SO SHABBY** (Boca Raton), and **THE PAINTED OX** (West Palm Beach).

Some of those shops also specialize in "beachy" or "coastal," as does **NEST** (Delray Beach), and **THE GOOD STUFF** (Jupiter). As for furnishings that are specifically old Florida/Palm-Beach-style (you know, the wicker rattan-tropical look), there's **CLASSIC FURNISHINGS** (Tequesta*)* **ELROY FURNISHINGS** (Delray) and **PALM BEACH REGENCY** (Lake Park).

WHERE TO FIND WEDDING DRESSES & BALLROOM GOWNS

Most resale shops only carry a few consigned ballroom-type gowns because they take up too much space. But here are a couple of shops which specialize in them: **TIMELESS ANTIQUES** (in back) (See Antiques Part III), **GUTSY GOWNS** (Delray Beach), and **ZOLA KELLER'S SECRET CLOSET** (see Broward County section).

Another (surprising) place where you can often find a few inexpensive wedding dresses (and ball gowns) is **WORLD THRIFT** in Lake Worth. On Wednesdays, everything is 50% off the color of the day for people over 55, and you can probably pick up a wedding dress quite cheaply. On the other hand, if you're over 55, you probably don't need a long white wedding dress.

WHERE TO BUY FURS IN FLORIDA

It has been said that the minute the temperature goes below 60 in Florida, women take out their furs and wear them to show them off. And some smart snowbirds choose to buy them in Florida where the prices are generally lower than in the north, especially at resales.

The best places where consigned furs can be found in the county are: **ANNEXE de LUXE** (Palm Beach), **CLASSIC COLLECTIONS** (Palm Beach), **CONNIE'S COLLECTION CONSIGNMENT BOUTIQUE** (West Palm Beach—Wellington), **DEJA VU (VINTAGE DEPARTMENT)** (Palm Beach Gardens), **ENCORE PLUS** (Boca Raton), **FASHION EXCHANGE** (Lake Worth), **SERENDIPITY** (Boca Raton), and **PARADISE LOST** (Palm Beach).

ဆာ၃

THE TEN BEST ONLINE SHOPS
FOR HOME DÉCOR

Stylist and decorator Kristin Cadwallader, who has a popular blog (bliss-athome.com) put together a list of her favorite online shops:

SHOP CANDELABRA www.shopcandelabra.com

SHOPTEN25 www.shopten25.com

ZINC DOOR www.zincdoor.com

LULU & GEORGIA www.luluandgeorgia.com

MINTWOOD HOME www.mintwoodhome.com ("the barware shop is a favorite here..." and they also "offer a custom pillow studio with designer fabrics")

ONE KINGS LANE www.onekingslane.com

FURBISH STUDIO ww.furbishstudio.com ("an awesome blue & white shop")

WAITING ON MARTHA wwww.shopwaitingonmartha.com,

DOMINO www.domino.com/shop

GILT HOME www.gilt.com/sale/home.

ဆာ၃

About the Author

"The Happy Shopper," **Paulette Cooper Noble**, lives in Palm Beach with her husband, Paul Noble, and their two Imperial Toy Shih Tzus, Polo (as in PoloPublishing), and Peek-a-Boo.

She has written 23 books (and over 1,000 articles) on a variety of subjects: *Bargain Shopping in Palm Beach County, Bargain Shopping in Fort Lauderdale, Broward & South Palm Beach, Palm Beach Pets & The People Who Love Them, The Scandal of Scientology, 277 Secrets your Dog Wants You To Know, 277 Secrets Your Cat Wants You To Know, The 100 Top Psychics & Astrologers in America,* and *The Medical Detectives.*

She is the winner of eight writing awards, and pens a regular pet column in the *Palm Beach Daily News.* Her bargain shopping credentials are: after college she once worked at Bloomingdale's for three hours so she could get the 20% employee discount.

For updates, go to FACEBOOK: SHOPPINGINFLORIDA

FOR MORE BOOKS BY PAULETTE, GO TO
PAULETTECOOPER.COM OR POLO PUBLISHING.COM

About the Editor

Paul Noble is a former television programming executive for Lifetime Television, Metromedia and Fox. In Palm Beach, he is on TV and film boards, and he would shop more frequently, but his wife has taken up all the closet space. He has co-written four books with her, and takes photos for their travel writing. He is co-President of the Circumnavigators Club with Paulette and the winner of five Emmys for producing and writing.

See www.paulrnoble.com.

About the Researchers

Lisa Peterfreund is a graduate of Yale University with her masters in environmental science. After a brief stint at Nordstrom's furthering her customer relations skills while enjoying discounts on merchant sales, she parlayed her expertise as a trustee of her small family foundation and now serves as philanthropic consultant for foundations and nonprofits.

Susan Coleman worked for Neiman Marcus and ran her own personal shopping business named "Shopping Unlimited." She saved her clients money by "bargain shopping" for them at places like Marshall's, T.J. Maxx, etc.

Andrew Fleschner, a Harvard graduate and investment advisor, is knowledgeable about antiques and assisted with the antique sections

Interview
With Paulette Cooper Noble
The Happy Shopper

When did you begin going to South Florida consignment and vintage shops? I lived in New York but my parents had a condo in Palm Beach and I visited them over the holidays. I found that the shops down here were better than the ones up north, so I raced to them whenever I came here.

When did you discover how good the resale shops down here are? My mother did volunteer work at a charity shop in Palm Beach. One day Ivana Trump's secretary donated five evening gowns worth $5,000 each—which they priced at $100 apiece. Mom called me to come over immediately, and after that, she began to call me to come over when something like a Hermes bag came in. I was hooked.

What made you write about these places? When I moved down here I had already written 15 books. I kept waiting for someone else to write a guide book to all these wonderful shops so I would know where to go, but no one did. So I figured it wouldn't be too much work (WRONG) because I was going to these places and knew them anyway.

Can't people get information about these shops free from the internet? That's what I thought at first. But when I tried to locate shops online, I found that so many of the listings were incorrect or incomplete. And it was frustrating to drive all the way to a shop that sounded great and find out that they had closed two years before. Plus, they don't give special shopping tour suggestions and maps. I do.

What extra information do you give people in this book that they can't easily find elsewhere? When the shops have special sales and where the sale merchandise is in the store, directions on how to get to some if it's complicated, shopping tour suggestions so people can go to a few great places in one area, and most important, what similar places are nearby. I always hated learning that I had missed a great consignment shop a few doors down while I was shopping at another one.

When did you begin consignment shopping? When I left college I lived at 80th Street between 5th & Madison Avenue in New York. ENCORE, the first real consignment shop, was at 84th & Madison. So I began going there—so frequently, that one of my friends commented that she didn't think I'd ever marry because there were no wedding dresses at Encore.

Why do you like bargain shopping? You've heard the expression: the pursuit of happiness? For many of us, it's the happiness of pursuit.

For updates, go to FACEBOOK: SHOPPINGINFLORIDA

124

NOTES

NOTES

NOTES

NOTES

CPSIA information can be obtained
at www.ICGtesting.com
Printed in the USA
LVOW01s2304080317
526617LV00006B/238/P